Tears & Laughter

A COUPLE OF DOZEN DOG STORIES

Tears & Laughter

A COUPLE OF DOZEN DOG STORIES

by
GENE HILL

Illustrated by
HERB STRASSER

PUBLISHED BY
PETERSEN PRINTS/LOS ANGELES

This is Marcia's book.
Much too little reward for all the tears
and
not nearly enough thankfulness
for all the laughter.

FIRST EDITION

ISBN: 0-8227-8039-9
Printed in the United States of America
Library of Congress Catalog Card Number: 81-82484

OTHER BOOKS BY GENE HILL
A Hunter's Fireside Book
Mostly Tailfeathers
Hill Country
A Gallery of Waterfowl and Upland Birds

"Trouble" and "Old Tom"
are reproduced from *A Hunter's Fireside Book*, by Gene Hill,
copyright 1972, by Winchester Press

CONTENTS

I REMEMBER seeing a poster in a country store many years ago that advertised a brand of chewing tobacco. I have forgotten the brand that was advertised, but I will never forget the poster. The poster, ancient when I saw it, pictured a stately gentleman of the era, wearing a full mustache and seated in a cane-bottom chair. A little girl sat in his lap and a young boy with an English Setter stood at his knee. The caption read: "A man who likes kids, dogs and a good chew of tobacco may not be a saint, but I'll bet on him." I was reminded of that poster as I read the pages of this heartwarming book. Gene Hill's stories and Herb Strasser's drawings together make powerful statements about the ancient and honored bond existing between man and dog. There can be no better blending of artistic talents.

Gene Hill's deeply moving stories have become the standard for modern outdoor writing. This book is a collection of his finest dog stories. They depict the very special place dogs hold in Gene's life as they are bred not only to be fine hunting companions, but to become respected and loved members of the family as well; not treated simply as prideful examples of some fine new hunting machinery. I first met Gene Hill through his stories, and I was very pleased to discover that he was the same amiable sportsman that I had come to know in his stories.

Herb Strasser's renderings of hunters and their dogs have likewise become standards in the sporting world. One now has "a Strasser" when he has a drawing of himself and his dog.

All of us cannot be fortunate enought to spend a day in the field with these men and their dogs, but reading this book is the next best thing.

Martin "Bubba" Wood
DALLAS, TEXAS
OCTOBER 1981

Brown dog

LATELY THERE'S BEEN an upsurge in the popularity of what's called the "versatile gun dog." The term covers several breeds, all European in origin. Now, while I'm not knocking any claims about them as such, I'd like to point out that this country has had such a dog for longer than I can remember. It's not really a breed; it's more of a type. I had one when I was a kid and nearly everyone else I knew had one at some time or another. You might call it a "brown dog."

Brown dogs are not really all brown. Some run a little orange in the coat and others have a pronounced grayish, but lackluster cast. Still, common brown is the predominant shade. The hair may be sort of long, though not necessarily, and can be either smooth or rough or in-between. They have a peculiar three-quarter sideways gait as if the front wheels are out of alignment, and they tend to use only one back leg at a time, resting one or the other alternately unless an emergency occurs requiring full power.

No farm can be said to be properly run unless there's a brown dog in some position of authority. They will herd cows and pigs, keep the chickens out of the house garden, and keep the area free from skunks— which accounts, in large measure, for their rather distinct odor. No boy can be properly raised without one.

I think it was Robert Benchley who once remarked, "Every boy should have a dog. It teaches him to turn around three times before lying down." Brown dogs do a great deal more than that. They provide excuses for adventures, teach him how to whistle loud and clear, improve his throwing arm, and, most important, instill in him the incredible responsibility that comes with being loved unquestioningly, totally, and irrevocably.

Brown dogs are famous for their nonchalant, sophisticated attitudes. They have an air of having seen it all before; an attitude of preoccupation. Mine would stop now and then and stare into middle distance, as if pondering some crucial question for a minute or so. Then having resolved it to his satisfaction, he'd shake his head as though wishing he could impart this gem of knowledge to me, but somehow feel it would be wasted or more likely that I simply would not understand its value.

The narrow achievements of ordinary gun dogs—pointers, setters, or retrievers—seem to amuse the all-capable brown dog. Anyone who has owned one knows that they will bring back anything they can carry or drag. They will turn a brush pile inside out for the rabbit hunter, or circle a squirrel tree at precisely the right pace and distance to put the squirrel just where you want him. Pointing birds seems to bore them, but get one working pheasants and he'll herd and flush them your way as easily as he'd run a pasture full of Holsteins back to the barn. For a farm boy who wants results—fried rabbit, or squirrel stew—the brown dog is guaranteed to get the job done.

A brown dog will tolerate a boy's family but will not get too involved. If the boy is absent, say during school days, he will mope around or curl up close to where the master will first appear upon coming home, and wait. If there are things he has to attend to, rounds to make or whatever, never doubt that the sound of the school bus will fall on his ears first and farthest away.

When the owner of a brown dog I know went off to

college, the dog would move out to the end of the lane about a day and a half before his pal was due home. How did he know? I haven't the foggiest idea. Since the boy's father didn't know when to expect him home either, it's even more mysterious—except that, if you're a brown dog, you're expected to know such things and it's your job to act on them.

Brown dogs are never trained in the common usage of words. They just figure out what has to be done and they do it. If you need someone to sit and listen to your problems, they'll lend a most sympathetic ear. If you're bursting with spring, they'll race up and down the brook with you and even walk a little taller when you bring mom the first sprigs of myrtle or watercress. I suspect they like summer best of all because everyone's home. Brown dogs are very fond of parties: swimming hole picnics, hayrides, summer softball games, fireworks, bicycling, fishing trips, and camping out. They make good outfielders and lifeguards, and I wouldn't have dreamed of sleeping on the lawn without my brown dog to watch over me; nor would he have allowed it in the first place.

Most problems with brown dogs stem from their intelligence and unswerving desire to please. Mine went along with me and my first .22 to watch me get rid of a few groundhogs in one of the pastures. I suppose I shot two or three; I forget. But he got the idea that we wanted groundhogs, and nearly every day, all that summer, he brought one home. The problem was that he didn't bring them home immediately, but waited a day or so until they were more impressive—in both size and smell. That little lesson wasn't lost to me either. I learned that there were certain outings to go on alone after that, especially when I was going to shoot snakes in the ice pond or around the place in the brook where we liked to swim. What would have happened if he had decided we wanted water snakes strung out on the porch? It still fills me with pangs of desperation.

One neighbor had to keep a chain around the kitchen icebox door after his brown dog learned to open and close it. It was a mystery where the food was going for a while, since he was smart enough not to take a lot or too big of a piece . . . just a small snack now and then to tide him over in the evening hours. Another had to tie the dog in the cellar or the barn if he felt he had to spank his son, and even then the dog would snarl a little at him for two or three days, as if to say he knew and didn't like the idea at all.

It's a shame that not everyone has a brown dog to help him over the rough spots, or to share that time of incredible wonder and discovery. A brown dog is a special gift we should have at a certain time of our life to round it out. A brown dog belongs to that time of life which was filled with dreams of what we see today as small things: a hammer .22, slingshots, a first knife of your very own, and hip boots; the little keys that opened the first doors to the outdoor treasures we now prize above price. Somehow brown dogs understand these things, and know how to share them.

I used to think, with pride overflowing, that my brown dog was mine. Now I know better. We never really own a dog as much as he owns us. Where he led I would follow without fear, and even now, remembering how he would curl up with his back against my bedroom door, I know again how it was to feel safe and protected from anything and anyone.

Once when I was very small and very sick my mother put him in bed with me against everyone's advice. "They need each other," she said, and that was that. She understood brown dogs and their peculiar magic.

It's getting about that time for another brown dog to come and live around the place. Sometimes I feel a strange cold draft at night. A brown dog would know just how to curl his back up against the door to keep it from troubling me.

The idler of March

MARCH IS kind of a good month for me. It's usually too cold and wet to do much in the way of outdoor chores and the women don't want me in the house underfoot. So I spend considerable time just hanging around.

It so happens that right now I'm lucky enough to be able to hang around a couple of black Labrador puppies who like to take me for long, rambunctious walks. Black cyclones at my feet, I am steered unerringly and with very few diversionary skirmishes, toward the brook.

If there is a place in heaven for Labrador Retrievers (and I trust there is or I won't go) it'll have to have a brook right smack in the middle—a brook with little thin shoals for wading and splashing; a brook with deep, still pools where they can throw themselves headlong from the bank; a brook with lots of small sticks floating that can be retrieved back to shore where they belong; a brook with minnows to play with; a brook with muskrats and muskrat holes; a brook with green herons and wood ducks; a brook that is never twice the same with surprises that run and swim and fly; a brook that is cold enough to make the man with the dog run like the devil away from his shaking; a brook with a fine spot to get muddy and a sunny spot or two to get dry.

At the end of the walk the puppies shrink into sleep like so many run-down toys. And I stand a minute or two and watch them. One lies on his back with his feet in the air like a bed turned upside down; the other two lie in more conventional attitudes. I feel a little younger just watching them, hoping they'll stay just like this a little longer, but I know how anxious they are to grow big enough to be unclumsy with their funny, outsized feet.

The old dog comes out now and stands watching with me, hurt that she wasn't invited along even though she's too old to stand the kind of roughhouse that the puppies put her through. She looks up at me, her eyes saying "please", and off we go the way we used to go together—except that a decade of time and all its little hurts have come to stay. I like to think that my old Tippy has her dreams of when she was young and strong with legs like Osage orange hunting bows. I'm more than sure she really knows we're getting old and just in kindness pretends to me we're not. She'll lug along a stick and once or twice she'll nudge it in my hand for me to throw—an old lady window shopping carrying her purse along in case she wants to give herself some little treat.

Where did our ten years go, my graying friend, my love? How unfairly fast the time has come when your body can't obey your great, great heart. No matter Tip, we were young together and knew what life was all about. Let's turn back now and build a fire and take a little nap.

A man can do some serious thinking while he's just hanging around, staying out from underfoot. I've got a lot of things that I've saved up for my midwinter spending. I know there'll come a span in life when all times seem like March. I'll lack the warmth inside me, then, to do much in the way of chores and no one will want me underfoot. But I'll always have some spots where I still like to hang around. There's a duckblind on the eastern shore where I once saw the canvasbacks tumble in the blocks so thick from a snow squall whistling on their heels. I couldn't shoot for fear of taking three or four with just one shot. Or I can hang around a little setter dog named Ben and chase a flight of woodcock through an ancient orchard sweet with the smell of northern spies and red fall pippins. I can walk along the ponds I used to trap when my grandpa bought my possums from me for a dime. I can find my dad and we'll just get old Red and hunt us up some coon when the misty night becomes moon-washed and soft.

I'll always have the Beagles, the pointers, the Redbone and Bluetick Hounds, the Labs, the setters and all the men that went with them. I'll have just the weather that I want—when I want it. I've got Chesapeake Bay and the Mississippi River. I've got the high Sierras and the Jersey swamps. I can break my first twenty-five again at trap with my old Model 12 and hang around the gun club for a while acting nonchalant about it.

Some of the best hanging around I do is in front of a fire. A fire gives a man something to care about. It's company. It keeps him busy. He can make it roar or gentle him. A good fire has it all: the smell of whiskey and apples and wet dogs; the colors of dawns he's loved and sunsets he's regretted. It's the best place to clean guns and make plans and remember stories.

Right now give me a good fire, some puppies to play with, and an old dreamy dog who likes to have her belly rubbed. March will be soon gone, pulling spring along behind, while we've just been hanging around.

The dog man

THE DOG MAN smokes his pipe and walks around staring at the litter of puppies. Years of experience have prepared him for this moment. He can recite the conformation and peculiarities of every fine dog of the breed. His careful study of the lineage of the sire and the dam and their sires and dams is reflected in his perceptive eyes. He is cold and unemotional because he knows that shortly he is going to pick a gunning companion that will be at his side for years. One of these seven-week-old puppies today brawling with its kin in the pen will shortly, by his urging and handling, fuse all its great instincts into The Perfect Dog.

He reaches in and hefts several of the puppies. He lifts their ears and they sink their little needle teeth into his fingers. He reaches into his pocket and brings forth a carefully preserved grouse wing—saved from last fall for precisely this moment. He unwinds the fishing line he has wrapped around it and trolls it through the boiling orange and white sea in the pen. They leap on the grouse wing and shred it. The Dog Man is delighted.

The choice is difficult. Suddenly in the midst of his weighty speculation, he feels an acute pain in his ankle. A young setter bitch has crawled out of the pile and bitten him. He brushes her away and she worries his trouser cuff. The Dog Man is concentrating on a frisky male wrestling with one of his brothers in a corner. The little female puppy is now into his shoelaces. He picks her up and she licks his face and snuggles into his arms. She has chosen the Dog Man. The visions of the young male on point fade as he shifts the sleeping puppy from one arm to the other to pay the man who runs the kennel.

All the way home the Dog Man drives very carefully because the pup has her head in his lap. His family, who has been waiting on the front lawn, watches as he holds up the pup and listens as he begins lecturing.

"This is a bird dog; an English Setter of the Laverack type. She is an orange Belton. She is not a toy nor is she to be a house pet. She is a hunting machine. She will live in the kennel."

Having made his speech the Dog Man puts the pup on the lawn and his family fondles it. An hour later the Dog Man is sitting in his study reading the chapter on puppies in *Gun Dog* for the fifteenth time. The puppy is asleep in his lap, stuffed to bursting with biscuits.

In six months the new doghouse is used to store kindling. The pup sleeps in the arm chair in the Dog Man's bedroom. His clothes are covered with orange and white hair. All in the family sneak goodies to the dog under the dining room table. The Dog Man severely admonishes them for this, even while doing it himself.

As time goes by the Dog Man will have acquired, at the very least, a set of whistles, a flushing whip, a bell for the dog's collar, training dummies, tubes of so-called quail and pheasant scent, various combs, brushes, shampoos, sprays, ointments and an assortment of leashes and ropes. The old doorknobs will have been replaced by new ones bearing likenesses of pointing dogs and upland birds. Coffee cups will arrive bearing similar motifs. The reliable family sedan has given way to a fancy station wagon outfitted with an expensive kennel. An array of packages and bottles containing vitamins and various dietary supplements will stand near the prepared-dog-food bag (whose contents he knows by heart, right down to

the percentage of carbohydrates and "fiber").

Expensive prints of dogs on point in Georgia, Alabama, Texas and the Carolinas will be arrayed on the walls. His wife will wonder why he never paid half that much attention to her or his children, but she will not say so out loud. She instinctively knows that a Dog Man does not have too much time in his life for trivial small talk. She will have to learn the difference between "breaking," "bolting" and "blinking."

If she needs a new winter coat she is more likely to get a pair of leather-faced brush pants and a matching canvas coat, two sizes too big, so she can attend field trials with him and look the part of the Dog Man's wife. (The most important thing for a lady to know about field trials is that they are held in the open and that there is no bathroom.)

In brief, the Dog Man is not like ordinary sane men. He is a subspecies whose habitat, language, working patterns, familial relationships and drinking styles set him apart. Scientific studies have indicated that this condition is irreversible and that he tends to throw similarly minded offspring.

I must confess that I am the same sort: a Dog Man. Dogs of all sorts of breeds have selected me with the uncanny instinct that a con-man has for a sucker. They spot me as undisciplined, self-indulgent, and addicted to indolence—in short, the perfect type of man for the average dog to own.

One of the problems afflicting the Dog Man is that, despite his subscription to all the field-trial news magazines, avidly reading every dog book ever printed and even having a fairly wide range of shooting experiences, chances are he seldom has the opportunity to see a really first-rate, fully-schooled, bird dog on the job and under his gun. He knows in theory what to expect but he rarely, if ever, has the blessed opportunity to be in on such a day in the field. The few relatively competent dogs that I've gunned over have trained themselves. Their owners claim to the contrary. A really good dog trainer is a man of infinite patience, understanding and skill. I'm convinced that more dogs are ruined by the lack of ability or knowledge and patience of a trainer to put himself in the position of the dog—literally and figuratively—than any other single thing.

And certain men have a way with certain kinds of dogs. My friend, Bill Wunderlich, is one of the finest professional trainers of retrievers. He knows how they are going to think before they do, and more often than not, Billy can anticipate a mistake and prevent it from happening, turning a possible negative experience into a positive one. To see him work a young dog is an awesome experience in human skill and understanding. Yet

Billy has a great fondness for pointers and by his own admission really just can't seem to break one himself and buys his pointing dogs trained.

My advice on dog training is generally worth just about what it costs, but here it is anyway. Don't expect more from a dog than you're willing to put into working with him. And to find out how much work it really is, make a point of seeing a field trail and finding out what a first-class dog can do—and talk to the man who runs the dogs. If you can afford it, and I think it's the least expensive in the long run, and if you're really serious about having a good dog, you're ahead by buying one fully trained or at least well-started.

It takes a lot of time to do it yourself—and by a lot of time I mean virtually every single day that's possible should have some time allotted to working your dog. If you're willing to devote that much time, fine. You'll have one of the most rewarding experiences of your life. But I'm heavily oriented toward the professionals. If I had the time I'd start out by spending as much time with the pros as I could, and expect to pay them for their advice and help. Most of them have seen more and forgotten more about dogs than you or I will ever dream of. I've read everything I could, but it's one thing to study up on handling a Labrador on a blind retrieve and something else to see Billy Wunderlich actually do it. I believe that a dog likes to be good at what he's supposed to do, that they understand discipline as much as they understand affection and that the two should be ladled out freely.

I remember training one of my Labradors to do a rather difficult series of retrieves which involved going from land through water, over land and through water again to find a bird that she hadn't seen shot. Time and again she fell short of what I expected and both her patience and mine were beginning to fray a lot more than just around the edges.

Just about the time I began shouting like a maniac, out of pure frustration, the dog came back to within a few feet of me and waited until I had calmed down and then, through the expression on her face, told me as plainly as if she could speak, that she didn't really understand what I wanted her to do and that if I could find some way of explaining it, she'd be pleased to do it my way. And that's finally what happened.

Nelson Sills, whom I consider to be one of the finest trainers and judges of retrievers, once put it much more succinctly to me after watching me mishandle a dog that was clearly the best one in the trial he was judging. "Gene," he said, "it's too damn bad that you aren't nearly as good at handling as your dog is at retrieving." His implication, and it was true, was that if I'd left the dog alone that particular time she would have won. Too many dog owners don't know when to stay out of the act. When in doubt, don't do anything until you know what you're doing. If I had a nickel for every time I've called a bird dog off a near-point or given a retriever a bad line because I didn't understand what was going on, I could buy a dog that is smart enough not to pay attention to me when I'm making an ass out of myself.

Take the time to know your dog. I've got four in my kennel right now and every one is an individual and every one has to be handled according to its own peculiarities. (The same way my wife handles me according to my own idiosyncrasies.) Be plentiful in praise for their successes and slow to condemn their faults.

I can't conceive of hunting without a dog. I just don't enjoy a day in the field without seeing the fun that a dog has in working. If I have to choose between leaving the gun home or the dog, I'll set out with the dog.

When all is said and done, the things we remember most about our dogs are their oddities. And I can say with full knowledge that nobody will fully agree with me, that English Setters have done more to drive Dog Man to the Jack Daniels jar than all the other breeds combined.

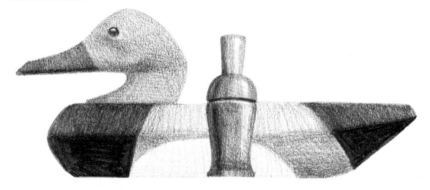

I once gave an English Setter puppy to my good friend, Bill Gray, the best veterinarian I know. Shelly instantly took over the good sofa, in spite of the lecture Bill gave his family and his initial intentions of establishing the mythical dog-master relationship. If Shelly were asleep on the sofa, shedding at a pretty good rate, everybody had to talk in a low voice and tip-toe around the room. I didn't understand why this was necessary because Shelly, like most dogs, was convinced that the ideal life was to sleep about 23 hours a day and reserve awake time for eating. Bill, of course, took her hunting and boasted constantly about Shelly's abilities as a woodcock dog in spite of the fact that Shelly never actually pointed the way dogs do in magazine illustrations. When she came up on a bird she'd just stop and stand there. I was convinced after seeing this that she was taking a little nap while Bill went about his business of flushing and shooting. In fact, this odd posture of hers was almost the undoing of Bill.

I met him on the street one day and asked him how Shelly was doing. "Just great," Bill said, and went down on his hands and knees in the street by my car to demonstrate how Shelly acted on a bird. He gave a perfect imitation, dropping his head down on his chest and closing his eyes and being so staunch that he came within an inch of being hit by a bread truck.

Even after a long year of force training, the only thing one of my English Setters would pick up without tortured reluctance was unbroken clay targets. Looking back on it, just this minute, I guess that's where she had the most opportunity.

Another little liver-and-white setter of mine was, not happily for me, completely convinced he could fly. I can see him now, carefully looking back on my rushing figure. He'd be low to the ground and wishing his way nearer the bird, when suddenly he would coil himself like a cobra and leap into the air at the exact moment the bird flushed, his teeth closing like knives on empty space, so full of another failure to soar he never heard my tattered throat roar whoa! In all fairness to his long-departed spirit (now somewhere, I hope, equipped with wings in some celestial bird field), Ben did catch one quail in flight. He delivered it to me without a scratch as if to say that he was right and I was wrong and that I had a thin outlook on his virtue of perseverence.

I had another setter for a while that was obsessed with a love for automobiles and was equally the most quickly and thoroughly carsick dog I've ever known. I couldn't drive 100 yards until it all came out. But no one ever drove in the driveway and got out of the car before she was in it. And like a lot of setters, she would eat anything this side of a charred stump. I've got to say one thing in her favor, she was fastidious about upchucking. Ordinarily a dog will just throw up, but not Tip. She'd get in the back seat, force her muzzle down in the crack between the cushion and the back of the seat, and then regurgitate.

A five-mile drive to the veterinarian was an adventure that needed at least 24 hours of preparation by fasting. But to give the devil his due, she always outsmarted us by saving something—Lord knows how—and never failed to make a little deposit. Hunting her was next to impossible. I couldn't drive anyplace because she had the areas for miles around the house so scoured out of birds that it was virtually pointless. She wasn't much bigger than a Holstein calf so we just kept her as a house pet. The cat taught her how to catch mice so whenever we heard a scream from a female guest or a muffled grunt of surprise from a male, we knew that Tip was running around the living room with a live mouse hanging by its tail from her mouth. Then with one great swoop of her tongue . . . she'd swallow it!

There are millions of fine-pointing, staunch-holding, turn-and-come-to-the-whistle bird dogs, and the remembered pictures of them standing tall and proud must be wiped from the eyes with a handkerchief. But the dogs that seem to stick even more sweetly in our hearts are the dogs that do it all a bit differently.

We know dogs that ring the doorbell when they want to come in and pull your hand when they want to go out. We know dogs that can count, appreciate dry bourbon Manhattans and sneer obviously when you fluff a crossing shot. If you live on 100 acres of weeded farmland, and plant just one expensive rose, we know where the dog will dig his next dusting hole. We know dogs that will not jump up on you in overalls but will bide their time until you're dressed up; dogs that will sleep on the floor of the car unless they're muddy and stinking; and dogs that will not throw themselves through a screen door unless it's new screening. Hunt with him by yourself and he's perfect; brag and hunt him in front of friends and he clowns.

Nobody can fully understand the meaning of love unless he's owned a dog. He can show you more honest affection with a flick of his tail than a man can gather through a lifetime of handshakes. I can't think of anything that brings me closer to tears than when my old dog—completely exhausted after a full and hard day in the field—limps away from her nice spot in front of the fire and comes over to where I'm sitting and puts her

head in my lap, a paw over my knee and closes her eyes and goes back to sleep. I don't know what I've done to deserve that kind of friend, but I'm humble enough not to ask any questions.

I once owned a dog that liked to smile at me and I took a great deal of pleasure in it—as she knew. When you're in the business of being man's best friend you have to develop a broad mind, some individuality and a strong sense of humor. I can't think of anything that would charm me more than someday having a dog that knew how and when to pass a wink my way—dog to Dog Man.

Daisy

LAST SUMMER I was picked out by a Brittany Spaniel. Although flattered, I don't really know why she chose me. I'm not particularly well conformed, my markings have no distinction and the less said about my bloodlines the better.

I didn't especially want to be owned by a Brittany at that time, but Daisy simply separated herself from the rest of her family and came over and sat on the toe of my shoe. When I jiggled my foot she bit my ankle to make me stand still. Obviously she knew more than a little about training people and shortly prepared herself to leave the Ohio home of my friend Tom Keast and move east to take care of me.

Here I will admit that I knew my wife would not be home when Daisy and I arrived from the airport; not be home, in fact, for several days, by which time I would have myself prepared for answering hard questions.

I leave it to your imagination as to the varying inflection and meanings possible in the phrase "What we really needed is another dog!" is roughly what my wife said when she arrived home after driving nine hours with the four dogs we already owned.

The prosecution and the defense stated their cases. Precedents were quoted from previous trials, most notably *Marcia Hill vs. New Trap Guns* (1954-73) and *Marcia Hill vs. Every Weekend At One-Or-Another Gun Club (1962-73)*. But since both of these cases are still under appeal, and the defense having noted that Daisy was now sitting on the toe of the prosecutor's shoe, this learned counsel declined to present further argument and rested the case. Exhibit A then bit the prosecution tenderly on the ankle. Prosecution stated that Exhibit A was probably hungry, picked her up and began offering bits of the defense counselor's luncheon hamburger. Exhibit A gently licked the face of the prosecutor, thus immediately changing status from Exhibit A to Daisy Hill—effecting immediate dismissal of the case.

Daisy soon traveled in the same casual circles of self-interest as the rest of the pack, with one exception. Instead of getting up on just any old furniture, Daisy likes the couches and chairs with fluffy cushions. When she gets in bed with one of the girls at night—the head rests on the pillow. Remarks were passed about. "Daddy's gun dog is asleep, so you can't sit on the good chair," or, "Do you think Daddy's gun dog looks cuter on the orange pillow or the brown ones?"

Let's let it go by saying that Daddy's gun dog is a little spoiled. Still the dream exists. As I see Daisy stretched out on the pillows on the couch it's not difficult to imagine a staunch point and a brisk retrieve. It's easy to conjure up the ideal picture of the eager worker and the skillful, confident trainer gradually honing the perfect relationship. And I have reason to believe it will happen as soon as Daisy grows up a little.

All of my gunning dogs, the setters, the Labs—and now Daisy, have been primarily house dogs. When you live with a dog you get to know its character. You see if the dog is shy or bold under a lot of circumstances. And, primarily, you can get in constant little periods of training. Dogs soon learn how serious you are by the tone of your voice. They get used to lots of other people and lots of other dogs. They learn that they are loved—and if that isn't important in training, I don't know what is.

By living with Daisy, I've learned that she is curious, imaginative, a little headstrong and as bold as a buck sergeant in boot camp. So I know that I can work her harder and more forcefully than I can a pup that's a bit soft, shy or indecisive. I know that any good professional would arrive at these conclusions in a tenth the time it takes me, but I have the privilege of time, and I like training my own dogs my own way. When I work a puppy or a young dog, I go by the positive method. I use very little coercion, seldom scold or shout. Instead I praise heavily when things are done right. When a dog is pleased at having learned something, so am I, and when a lesson goes sour, I return, for a little while, to the things that the dog *can* do, to keep her confidence up. If a training session seems like it isn't going anywhere at all, I've learned to stop everything and rethink it myself to find out if there is another way to get the idea across to the dog.

A good example is the problem of getting some dogs to work through really harsh cover—briers, for instance. One way that works for me is to get in there and go through them myself and have the dog follow. By doing that I make a little path for the dog, and she learns that it isn't as bad as it looks, and after a while the dog learns to pick her own way through. I won't send a dog into the water unless I've checked the area where she will enter, to make sure it isn't too shallow, stumpy or harboring anything that can hurt the dog.

You really have to learn how your particular dog thinks and how things look from the angle of the dog—who is considerably lower to the ground than you are. You have to learn not to get excited and give contradictory orders like shouting "back" while giving the hand signal for "over."

Contrary to a lot of training techniques, I don't like to start working a dog with any serious intent until it is used to the gun and I've taken a couple of birds that the dog has put up—and I don't mean birds I've flushed when the dog is around—but birds the dog has really worked and been involved with. There is no way that I know of to train "hunt" in a dog. Either your dog is enthusiastic about the whole thing, or you're stuck. And when dogs know what the whole thing is about, you're ready to teach them to do it your way. It may take me a little longer this way, but in the long run I think I end up with a more eager dog.

I hunted over dogs that were trained out of their love for the sport, and I didn't much enjoy it—no matter how efficient they were. And I've wasted a lot of time with some wild streaks of lightning, but good, bad or in-between, I can't imagine being afield without one.

I can't imagine living in a house without a couple of dogs. If I ever got out of bed at night and didn't have to step over a Labrador or two or three, or move one off the covers so I could turn over, my nights would be more restless and the demons that wait in the dark for me would be less easily fended.

Bringing Daisy into our family was an introduction of youth into the lives of everyone. The old dogs had someone to romp with and quarrel with over sticks. The kids had something to spoil, and the old man could pull out an old dream and give it a little polishing. Bird covers are looked at with new interest, and the possibilities of a new upland gun, one befitting the latent talents of a tousled-eared orange-and-white lady Brittany, are again up for legitimate consideration.

After the training birds have come and gone, and the swamp maples decorate the springy bottomlands with yellow and orange and red, we'll sit on the edge of the meadow at evening and watch for the first dusking flights of woodcock to flicker across the autumn sky. I can see us now, slipping easily into the slow and careful pace of the watchful gunner and the thorough dog—and then at Daisy's first tentative point of a bird that she has never known, I step in, do my part and wait as Daisy proud-trots back and puts the woodcock in my hands.

It won't happen, but I wish it would, that we might start out the gunning season in the North and stay with the flights for thirty days or so—throw in a partridge now and then to give us both a little change of pace—until the birds have passed by close to home.

It seems a shame that a man and his dog so rarely get the time to spend together that they'd like—doing what they both like best. A man isn't born to too many gunning seasons, and his dog is offered but a handful or so to spend with him before it's time to say good-bye . . . leaving a photograph or so slipped in a favorite book and a memory of special days.

I can't, in any conscience, ask Him for special favors, but on that day this fall when Daisy stands to her first woodcock and I walk in past that little dog, I'd sure give thanks for a small clearing in the cover and one more little thing, Lord—please make it a straightaway.

Old Tom

THE VET told him the old dog might live a week or so and that the humane thing to do would be to put him down. The man brushed his moustache with the back of his hand so that his fingers covered up his eyes and said he didn't believe he was ready to do without Old Tom right now. Maybe in a day or so, but not right now.

So the two of them shuffled out to the car and drove off. Now the old man had a problem. It was mid-March and bird season was long since closed. But more than he'd ever wanted anything, he wanted the dog to hear one more shot and feel the whirr of one more flush.

March or not, the old man took a vigil near the swamp that night and marked down two or three birds coming in to roost. At six the next morning the two gentlemen marched down together as they had done countless times before . . . and as one of them hoped they would do countless times again in some other field.

The play was faultless. Old Tom drew himself up as proud as a puppy. The old man's shot was as true as a youngster's and the deed was done.

At the vet's a half hour later, his last bird cradled between his front feet, his nostrils filled with the scent of what he had lived for, Old Tom went to sleep.

The old man lets him rest up on a hillside facing the western sun. And on the slate that marks the spot he scratched "OLD TOM. A Faithful Friend For 12 Fine Years". On fair days, when no one is watching, the old man goes up to the slate and sits in the sun with a glass of whiskey and talks about times past with Tom.

The cycle

I HAVE LONG BEEN land-poor for the simple reason
that I keep Labrador Retrievers. Labs require water and
that means a pond. Ponds cost money which I have little
of, hence the current situation. I don't know where the
expression "going to the dogs" originated, but it might
very well signify a trip to the poorhouse. I have enough
common sense not to add up veterinary bills, the outra-
geous price of dog meal, kennel licenses, practice ducks
and the other odds and ends—including the interior of a
station wagon which one of the dogs tore to shreds in
something less than five minutes. Nor do I add in shoes
that were preferred to the store-bought rawhide sticks
and nylon bones for teething exercise, or the Christmas
lights and ornaments, when one of the puppies got tangled up in the cord and upset the whole tree.

Someone who doesn't own dogs (and who might
even have such a thing as a savings account) could wander around our place and tote up training pistols, blank
shotgun shells, training dummies, dummy launchers,
check cords, collars, leashes, even the kennel itself and
come up with a figure that would make the average duck
retrieved worth about the same as a race horse. (I almost
forgot to add in a velvet-covered rosewood sofa that one
of the dogs felt would be more comfortable if the stuffing
were adjusted a bit differently from how the manufac-
turer had chosen.)

I guess we feel the same way about dogs that J.P.
Morgan felt about yachts—if you have to ask how much
they cost, you can't afford to own one. I don't think three

or four dogs cost more than a yacht, but then I never asked either.

The point of all this is that I'm trying to rationalize the fact that I'm taking another dog into the family. If you grant that two can live as cheaply as one, then certainly you must applaud the logic that five can live as cheaply as four. The casual non-dog-owning observer might look around my tattered Eden and remark, thoughtfully, that it doesn't look as though I *need* another dog. But then, what would he know about why a new dog is needed?

Among the more important reasons a new dog is needed is that my old dog, Judy, is not long from leaving us. Her deep brown eyes are now misted with age; her rising up to meet me, as eagerly as ever, is difficult and painful for her to accomplish, and almost unbearable for me to watch. She needs a new puppy to play with, and so do I—for just about the same reasons.

An acquaintance was going on the other day about being too old to take on a puppy to train. Of course I disagreed, but for reasons of my own. I assume his ideas of training are somewhat different from mine—or at least the results are.

History has shown that I am more likely to be the trainee than the other way around. Puppies quickly discover that my bark is worse than my bite and that I can be taught to do tricks. They learn that I sleep better when there's a dog at the side of my bed, and that I am willing to feed them, more or less surreptitiously, if they sit under the table by my chair. I can be charmed into tomfoolery with a tennis ball, and this old catcher's arm is still good enough to count on for retrieving games in the pond.

Puppies seem to know that one of their functions is

to make time stand still—they are not only another beginning themselves, but they have a way of spreading it
around making everybody feel a little younger.

Every dog I've ever owned can easily be recalled to
mind. Each had a most distinct personality—a set of
quirks, a philosophy, an individual attitude toward life.
Some were clowns and some somber as owls. Others
were con artists, chicken thieves or street-corner loafers.
Most were worth just barely passing grades as gundogs—

I'd say a C-. One setter might have been superb, had I
not ruined him, and two of the Labs I'd have to rate
around A, counting a little forgivable prejudice.

And that's much of the fun of a new puppy. You
wonder if it will grow up to be President, or if it will be
satisfied with an ordinary nine-to-five job. Some suddenly turn up indomitable while some shrink from obstacles
that others never even give a second thought. Some are
mean and selfish, others like unto the salt of the earth.

It's the rare exception that we can ever fully understand. We all know of good dogs who suddenly become gun shy, or gentle dogs turning mean. Barring some sickness which usually comes quickly to light, I find that these changes are, as often as not, purely mysterious.

None of my dogs ever came from a broken home, had any parental conflicts, or seemed upset at my having an occasional drink. I provided them with the best I could, taught them decent manners, bought them plenty of toys and gave them the benefit of all my worldly experience. Yet, several did not do me proud. If I failed somewhere, as surely I must have, I know not how. I saw their brothers and sisters being praised rightly for their virtues, and mine—well, sometimes the less said the better. Others were the kind you could take to church and be proud of and, as for me, I treated them all the same.

My mother once told me that she didn't believe much in trying to "train" children. She felt they were like horses—if they had the instincts of a thoroughbred they'd turn out all right; if they didn't there wasn't all that much she could do about it.

I believed she was right then, and I haven't changed my mind all that much about it. I've adopted her theory in raising both my dogs and my children—not wholly sparing the rod, and completely believing in innocence until shown otherwise beyond a shadow of a doubt. If a dog doesn't want to hunt, I know of no way to force him.

I'd give a lot if my old dog could help raise the young one. If only she could impart her sense of loyalty, her good nature, her incredible desire to make me happy and her almost unbelievable drive in the gunning field. But on the other hand, I don't think I'll ever belong to the ideal dog—nor should I. I'll be perfectly satisfied right now with the fire and warmth that comes rolled up in a puppy. As our own light grows dimmer and the cold more piercing with the coming of our winter years, a puppy brings us days full of sunrises and the promise of long and soft afternoons . . . that's all we can ask and all we really need.

One

I ADMIRED THE DOG out of courtesy and that was about it. He wasn't anything special to look at—just your nice, solid, big-headed black Lab. I've seen hundreds just like him, give or take an inch here or a detail there. His work in the field was efficient, but not exciting. He wasn't what a real trial man would call steady and as often as not he'd drop a goose to readjust a hold; generally preferring to drag it along by a wing. He did have one peculiar habit I noticed—he never picked up a bird, no matter how dead it was without stepping on the neck with one foot first and holding it there until he'd grabbed the wing. I asked about this, and his owner told me that it was a habit he'd had from the first, since his first goose had picked him pretty bad. This bit of cause and effect reasoning pleased me being a "once burned, twice shy" person myself.

This day in a goose pit on the eastern shore of Maryland was as common as the surrounding mud. Intermittent flights had us calling, more for the amusement of it than any real hope of turning them. But every so often a pair or a small flock of five or six would toll close enough for a shot and since we were in no hurry or that anxious to take geese, we took turns gunning. By mid-afternoon we each had two geese—enough for our personal satisfaction, but the weather was mild so we had come to a mutual unspoken agreement to just sit there and chat rather than pick up and go our seperate ways. It was a lovely way to spend an afternoon—gunning talk mostly, a little fishing talk, some book titles exchanged—just your average small talk between two relative strangers who found common ground and an occasional bit of laughter that sweetened the conversation putting each of us at ease and wanting the other to find us good company . . . a small, pleasant spontaneous friendship.

He hardly mentioned his Lab, and neither did I, but I was pleased to notice that the dog sat leaning a little against his masters leg or put his head on his foot when he chose to lie down, and that my companions hand was stroking the dog or messing with his ears or scratching him behind the neck. It was just the sort of thing any one of us might do, an ordinary circumstance, a common-place relationship. Nor did I find it strange that the dog paid absolutely no attention to me whatsoever. There are dogs that are nuisances for affection (several of mine were like that from being spoiled and encouraged to play) and others that like to keep to themselves, and others that are clearly one person creatures.

He had not bothered to bring a lunch, and I, for once, had gotten myself together and packed one. As usual, when I do get the lunch-making urge, I tend to go overboard and had more than enough to share, which I gladly did. We each had two sandwiches, and as he ate his he fed the other to his dog at the same pace, bite for bite. A sandwich and a half was enough for me, so I offered the dog the half left over. He wouldn't touch it from my hand, so I placed it on the floor of the blind in front of him where it sat unnoticed and untasted until I asked my friend if the dog were on some sort of self-imposed diet.

"No, I don't think so," he laughed, and picked up the food and as before fed it to the dog bite by bite.

You can usually sense when someone has been waiting for a chance to talk about something that needs to be aired. You feel that he's been looking for the right time and place and ear. I was hoping that I'd have that privilege, so I just sat there and watched him dribble pieces of that sandwich, pieces about the size of 00 Buck, to a dog that was not only used to this little game, but so delighted with it that he was making soft moaning noises and rolling his eyes like a fundamentalist convert.

"Pete, here, is about the worst dog I've ever owned," he said with some hesitation, "but he's taught me more about dogs, in a strange way, than most of the others I've had—and there have been quite a few."

I just sat there and stared at the floor of the blind, not wanting to look at him, because he didn't want to look at me . . . right now he wanted a listener, a sympathetic and understanding one—one who had some knowledge of what he was talking about, but not a conversation—just the ear would do fine for the time being.

"If you've ever followed the big field trial circuit you'd probably know my name. For quite a few years I was the amateur trainer that most of the pro's worried about. And they had good reason. I had the money, the time, the drive and the dogs. And you needed all that just to start because you were in against the Belmonts, the Roosevelts, big steel money, big oil money and just plain money so big that hardly anyone remembered where it all had come from. One handler drove his dogs to the trials in an old Rolls Royce fitted up like a kennel truck; the people he worked for drove Rolls' and they didn't want their dogs in anything less! I didn't go that far . . . but I wasn't too far behind. I've charted more than one plane to take my dogs where I thought they ought to be running and I never regretted a penny of it.

"I even had Purdey make me a pair of side-bys just for field trial gunning in case my dogs didn't finish so I'd still be part of the action—and you learn a lot about certain dogs when you're a gun—but that's getting a little away from my story.

"It all started simply enough—and typically as far as I'm concerned. I've always loved competition—I've been a top flight amateur golfer, a tournament winner on the trap and skeet circuit, and got to where they knew I was there in the live bird rings of Madrid and Monte Carlo. Then I got to thinking about getting a dog. I traveled so much in my early days that owning one didn't make much sense. My hosts, when I went shooting, all had fine kennels so it didn't make any difference if I had any or not. In fact it was better that I didn't. But when a big holding company bought me out for more money than I could ever spend and moved me up to some spot that was all title and no work, I began to look around for something new to take up. It was just about destined that I'd start field trialing Labs.

"I'd been a member of one of those fancy Long Island duck clubs for years and had seen some pretty good dogs. It might sound silly, but I believe that a man has to have a dog and a breed of dog that suits his personality. If I believed in reincarnation I don't doubt that I'd come back as a Lab—or would like to. It's a little vain I know, but I saw myself as brave, honest and strong, as Hemingway might have put it, and that's what I like about the Lab. It's all up front, nothing held back.

"Anyway, one of my duck hunting buddies at the old Sprig Club had a litter of dogs out of good field trial stock and he gave me a male as sort of a retirement present. He said that at worst he'd be somebody I could talk to and take care of and get the same in return. After I'd spent a few weeks with the pup I decided to have a professional take a look at him. I felt that he might have what it would take to be a trial dog, but I believe in the opinions of the people who do it everyday, not just an amateur appraisal.

"The professional not only liked the dog but made an offer then and there to take him for training, and I

agreed. He had a fine reputation and I liked his whole approach to the training idea. He was to start the dog, and when he was satisfied I'd come down and spend a week or so with him and learn to run the dog myself. Then I'd get a training schedule to work on and check back with him for a few days on a regular basis. If the dog did exceptionally well, he'd take him over completely and campaign in the major stakes. His name was Wonderdog—because I wondered what I'd do with him when I first got him; a little joke with myself. If you follow the retrievers you know how far he got and what a piece of pure bad luck it was he didn't become National Champion. He was killed a little while after his first Nationals—an assistant trainer was in an accident and the dog trailer was totally demolished. I was hurt by the loss, of course, but by then I'd been committed to try for another dog as good as he was. He'd sired a litter and I arranged to get the pick for stud service.

"If anything, he was better than his father; a bit more aggressive and strangely a bit more biddable. It was almost as if he felt destined to compete and understood what was expected of him all along. I called him Little Wonder—another private joke with myself. Almost everyone was soon calling him One, short for number one because that's what he looked like right from the start. He was one of the hottest derby dogs anyone had seen when he was right, and he usually was. I'd never thought of a dog as an athlete before One, but when he took to water he reminded me of a diver—I know it's silly to think of a dog having "form" but he did—and I never got over the idea that he knew it and worked at it.

"By the time he was three, One had totally captivated the trial circuit—not just in wins and placements, but by his personality—his pure competitiveness and genius for doing just the right thing at the right time. I know for sure that more than one judge laid out a series with just him in mind, but as hard as they tried to challenge him he was usually up to it. Of course he had an off-day now and then, disinterested or bored or maybe tired, but even then he did his job, but without the fire he was famous for. In his first National at Bombay Hook he placed third. I don't think he deserved to win, but I think he deserved at least second. The head judge and I weren't exactly friends, since I'd beaten his dog at several important trials and he wasn't above playing a little politics with some nationally known names.

"I'd planned to retire One after his first in the Nationals, and just use him as a stud dog and gunning companion. We'd become pretty close and I thought he deserved a little rest and some fun—and some of the fun

had gone out of the competition as far as I was concerned. But I did want that win for him in the worst way.
He'd worked hard for it and most of us still believed that
he had the class and the talent to go all the way; if any
dog deserved it, One certainly did. The more we worked
him that season the sharper he got. I didn't think that
there was much room for improvement, but in subtle
ways he just looked better. His long blinds were preci-

sion itself and when he was stopped to the whistle he really *stopped*. It was as if he were reading your mind—I
heard one judge remark in a friendly way that he looked
as if he were showing off. I'm making him sound as if he
were absolutely perfect, but he did have one small fault.
Not in every trial, but every now and then for some reason he'd make one or two little yelps on a retrieve on
land. I always put it down as pure enthusiasm and the
trainer and I had long given up trying to make him stop.

More often than not, we'd be the only ones to notice it."

Here he paused for so long I didn't think he was going to go on with the rest of the story. He was rumpling his dog and searching for the right words and the strength to say them. I had the feeling that this was a story that he'd never told before and perhaps didn't want to—yet knew that he must so he could get a different grip on it himself. For some strange reason I thought of the words to an old song about "hanging your tears out to dry"—how perfectly put, how perfectly true.

For the first time since he'd begun, he turned to look at me and I could see the gray, sad sparkle of small tears. I turned away a bit to give him a moment of privacy. He covered his face with his handkerchief for just a second and went on.

"I'd say the chances of what happened ever happening are more than one in a million. One of those random tragedies that always seem to strike the innocent; the casual passerby. There was a strand of wire, just one, that was only about two feet long between an old post and a tree. I'd heard One making his odd yipping noise and suddenly he went end over end in the air and lay still. Both the judges and I rushed out knowing instantly that something fearful had happened, and there was One stretched out, dead from a broken neck. A small trickle of blood ran down the corners of his jaw where he'd run into the wire with his mouth open.

"I carried him back to the station wagon and put him on the front seat and started to drive. I don't remember how long it was or where I went, but I do remember that I kept rubbing his head believing for the longest time that he'd suddenly sit up and everything would be all right. Today is the second time in my life that I've cried; that was the first.

"There's a small graveyard behind the lodge at the Sprig Club where our special dogs were put to rest and the whole club turned out to help me put him there. I had a blanket made of his ribbons and my gunning coat was his pillow. He always loved to sleep on that whenever he had the chance. One of the members read a list of his wins and when finished with that, he paused, and in a soft tenor began to sing Auld Lang Syne and everyone, except me, joined in with him."

He stopped again for a minute and blew his nose; I must confess I did the same.

"I virtually stopped gunning for a long time after that. When people asked me why, I told them that my favorite partner had passed away and almost none of them ever thought that it might have been just my dog. Funny, isn't it, how few can understand the relationship a man can have with his dog? And yet, I can tell you now that there were few, if any, things in my life that meant as much to me as One, and how odd but true that an emptiness like that is there forever.

"It's been about five years since I lost One and last fall a friend of mine, the same one that sang that afternoon at the duck club, came to my house and rang the bell. When I opened the door he reached in and put a puppy in my arms and said, 'It's about time Pete had someone to look after,' and turned and left."

"This is Pete." At the sound of his name Pete looked up and made some sort of a face that I'll say was as close to smiling as a dog can get.

"When I said that Pete was the worst of my dogs I didn't mean anything but that I'd never trained him. I just let him be Pete. And that's been enough, more than enough. They say that a man deserves one good dog in his life . . . but that's not true. I've had a couple, and in his own way, Pete's right there in my heart with them all now. It's a full space with two empty ones beside it if you can see it that way."

I nodded to let him know that I agreed, but I didn't say anything because I didn't think anything needed to be said just at that moment.

He began, after a little while, to talk about something else and after giving me his card he thanked me for listening and said it was time for him and Pete to be heading on home. I said goodbye and told him that I'd wait here a little while longer in the blind just to watch the sun come down. But that wasn't the whole truth. What I wanted to do was sit there in the quiet of twilight and hear the soft phrases of that ancient Scottish melody again in my mind and picture the scene of that group of men singing a dog to eternity and comforting themselves in the timeless ritual of shared sorrow and the understanding of loss.

In the last light, I slung my two geese over my shoulder and started back to where I'd left the car. I found myself softly singing what I could remember of One's funeral song, and surprisingly, I wasn't as saddened by the idea as you'd imagine. The saving thought was one of remembrance; as long as a man lives, so will his dogs in one form or another . . . in a story or a song. One will always be there to take care of the other and I can't think of a nicer way to put it than we will "share a cup of kindness now . . . "

Seven classic ways
to ruin your gun dog

IN MEDICINE one of the basic precepts is "do no harm"—don't make the patient worse. In dog training the basic precept is don't let the dog make mistakes in the first place. But so many of the "mistakes" that dogs make are not his fault—but simple reactions to what his handler does. Having committed most of these myself I feel very free to speak—it was ignorance and inexperience that made me do them—or lack of common sense.

But I'll bet that a lot of people you hunt with, as well as yourself, are guilty of one or more of these "NO's":

1. *Hunting too fast:* Even when a dog has established a distance he likes, you can force him to be a "Lone Ranger," simply by hunting at a pace that is yours— not his. Don't let him potter over every mouse track, but don't force him into the next county by being impatient—or distrustful. Chances are you'll pick up more birds as well.

2. *Talking too much:* Constant chattering to a dog teaches him to ignore you. The human voice also makes birds very edgy and the chances of good dog work are diminished. I've seen a rock-steady dog constantly admonished to be STEADY, HOLD'EM, WHOA THERE! Since a dog's vocabulary is less than William Shakespeare's you're only distressing him. Give him the benefit of the doubt.

3. *Inane commands:* There are times when a dog can't hear you and won't listen. To try to make him come in or sit or quarter when you know very well he won't

is only going to lessen his willingness to obey. Think the situation out and then react. *Go to the dog,* if possible, and only command when it makes sense—not out of ego or showing off. Especially with a young dog, only make demands when you can enforce them! Included here are things like suddenly saying KENNEL at the rear of your station wagon when you've never done it before. If you're going to spring a new command on him do it under the correct circumstances. And if you're going to teach a new command, don't do it twice and then forget it for a month and expect him to remember.

4. *Walk up straight behind a dog on point:* Why they do this in so many photographs I don't know. It may not bother a very experienced dog, but a young dog gets very nervous and edgy. He wants to see you and know where you are as much as the other way around. Come into your birds from the side. You'll get better shooting and your dog won't have the tendency to bump birds. Walking in straight behind him seems to force him into the birds—just what you don't want.

5. *Let other gunners handle your dog:* It's your dog and other gunners ought to know enough to leave the driving to you. If they find your dog on point they should let you know so you can handle the scene the way the dog is used to seeing it handled. Don't let them start giving strange commands or petting or playing with your dog in the field. Get this talked out before the hunt—it'll save a lot of friendships and be a big favor to Old Susie.

6. *Losing your temper:* I've seen some brutal things happen to a dog when it wasn't the dog's fault—just a man showing off or being stupid. I assume you're stronger than Old Susie. You don't have to prove it to me.

There are proper and necessary times to correct a dog and some take a little more convincing than others, but scaring an animal half to death is not part of any trainer's technique.

7. *Expecting too much:* I've seen retrievers sent on half-mile pick-ups in a heavy chop that would discourage a man in a boat—just the owner showing off by half-killing the dog—and six-month pups will likely see a bad going-over when sent to cope with a wing-tipped Canada or a barely scratched cock pheasant.

   Don't expect all dogs to be good retrievers. Some like it, some don't.

   Don't ignore your dog for months and expect him to remember where you left off in training or manners.

   Don't throw him into a new situation and expect him to handle it flawlessly—like running pheasants with a dog that's only seen quail. Give him time and give him the benefit of the doubt.

   Don't ignore weather conditions that affect hunting abilities or the fact that a dog gets hot and tired and thirsty and sometimes plain bored or disinterested.

A man has a great responsibility when he takes on owning a gun dog. You have to train yourself. You have to learn new things about birds and covers and weather. Don't expect every dog to be super—not one in five hundred is—or even close to it. Learn what a dog can do well and work around that even if it means altering your hunting techniques a little.

Learn to be patient—learn to think—and try to please him in some small degree as much as he's trying to please you. DON'T MAKE IT HARD FOR HIM TO DO THE BEST HE KNOWS HOW!

Stove side

YOU SIT AROUND and listen to the oldtimers talk, and if you watch their eyes, you see something magical take place. In the course of the chatter and the "remembering when" you watch the hands fly up swinging the ghosts of Parkers and L.C.'s; they suddenly take on the look of men of younger years. And every so often their hands reach down to pat a dog that's no longer at the side it kept for many years.

The ghost guns and dogs, partridges, quail or woodcock come alive in their eyes for a story and then fade away to rest until they're needed one more time.

When you stop to think about it, it's stories like these that hold the whole thing together. It's the passing down of times that constitute the glue, the living chain that binds us to the Old Fisher Farm orchard or the Bear Swamp, which none of us really remembers. But it takes on a reality that is almost painful in its absence.

The paths we walk, past corncribs to the meadow spring where the orchard started, become as clear as if we'd just been there ourselves. We listen to the arguments about the apples and almost feel as if we ought to take a side and go along with Bill or Tom and swear that we agree they were Pound Sweets or Northern Spies or Russets. Somehow it seems important to get these things decided right so every piece that follows drops into its proper place.

Someone goes back to the time when he cut the chestnut for the split rail fence that edged the cover where the very first fall of woodcock arrived like clockwork every year. We watch his hands place the wedges in the trunks again and see in his fluttering shirt where broad bands of muscle once pulled taut against his back. We feel the satisfaction of the sweat, and of seeing at the end of day, a line of neat-laid wood that, "By God would be there yet if they hadn't pulled it down to build the road that spoilt the best damned cover in the county!"

It's hard for me to watch these legends gun their country yet another time from stove-side and not feel some tremendous sense of loss. One talks now about how he "give everything away."

"Just got tired of seeing my old Baker sit around knowing me and it was through. Give it away for fifty dollars same as I paid, and when the man come for it I made him take my coat and vest; no mor'n rags to him, I know, heavy 6's in the left side and light 8's in the right; even half a can of P.A. from when I had teeth enough to hold a pipe. Let me swing her one more time, I told him, and then I turned her loose. He'll never know the deer and fox and birds I warmed them muzzles on and no reason for him to even care, but better for just one of us to rust away than both."

The talk drifts back and forth about guns and shots and days and seasons. Men who, a few hours ago, would have stumbled over the names of their children, recall with detailed accuracy barrel lengths, chokes, favorite loads, and shells and bags from fields and forests that have long been buried under asphalt and concrete. I waited for the other half of the team to be brought back to take their places weaving with high and proud heads in front of these hammer and hammerless paragons.

This is hard for most of them and I know it, but I know, too, how pride will conquer grief.

"The day I took them thirty partridges was a week

after Rufus's third birthday. He was bred out of Jingle Bell and Domino, both good dogs but a touch hard headed and I knew I could make something out of one of those pups and I got me one. My wagon had a bad wheel and I was a day or so late in getting over to Will's where they was and he only had the two left. One was a big hellion of a reddish cast and he was chewin' on his little sister like to drive her crazy. I says I'll just teach you some manners and fetched him home. The first thing I done was to cut a switch from that peach tree that used to be right outside the kitchen door and told him that there was plenty more where that come from and I meant to use them all if need be."

We all waited while he lit his pipe.

"Well, that little fellow looked at me, crawled under the kitchen stove, and went to sleep. I ain't ever used that switch on him to this very day."

And so it goes. Old Rufe is gentled into his mastery. Gipsy and Laura are compared (carefully and with tender thought—giving all concerned the benefit of the doubt) with Missy and Freckles and Jo. Each tells how he cured this one of gun-shyness, that one of blinking . . . suggestions made and noted about what to do with dogs that will never be.

I mentally turn them all into dogs: rib-sprung Will, a flashing pointer: soft-spoken Marvin, a delicate step-

ping setter; Henry, a wide-eyed Beagle . . . the kind that always seems close to tears. And then I turn them back again, my mind still questioning who ought to be the Gordon, the Springer, or the trumpet-throated Redbone.

I'm wrong and I know it; days weren't easier then. They worked themselves into old age at fifty or so. They struggled on with hurts that we wouldn't tolerate a day and kept right on because that's all the choice they had unless you think that hunger, or broken pride, or letting the bank have back the farm is a choice. I know all this is so, but for a little while I want to ignore it.

I want to remember them in clean bib overalls and red bandannas dancing to "Turkey in the Straw," and seeing their great thick hands holding a hymnal and hearing them, with honest believing voices sing, "The Old Rugged Cross," with their eyes fastened as far upward as their consciences would allow. I want to remember them arguing about who made the best hard cider and why Parker's were better than L.C.'s, and Gordon's better than Irish. I want to remember them as they remember themselves—young, strong and a little wild.

I watch their hands. Hands that could gentle a pup, upset a yearling bull, shave an eighth of an inch off an oak plank with an adze, and roll a cigarette without spilling a speck of Bull Durham.

I watch their eyes. They could see a boy's mischief through a barn wall, stop a dog in its tracks, make a young school teacher blush, or put an ounce of 7's right in front of a partridge.

I want them thirty years old again, and I want to be there with them. I want a hammer gun just like theirs and a pair of soft-footed setters. I want to ride in a wagon or a Model A truck and walk the land their grandfathers wrestled first from the Indians . . . and then from King

George. I want to be there on the day they brought home sixty woodcock and forty grouse.

But it is not to be. Before long the chairs by the wood stove will be empty, the men gone to join their dogs, leaving us only a thread of memory and a lingering sorrow and loneliness.

These old men, who had a foot in each century, were a bit uncomfortable toward the end. They were part ghost, and they knew it. Their familiar tools were becoming antiques. Their skills and the pride in them were taken for curiosities. Who is left to teach us how to hitch up a team of horses—common knowledge to all of them—or find a bee tree, or shave a spoke for a wheel? Who is left for us to measure ourselves against in that common-to-all-of-them standard of self-sufficiency?

Who so have we left to sing the old songs and tell the stories that brought our great uncles and grandfathers back to be with us? Who is still here to tell us, with the passion of face-to-face, about the passenger pigeon, the woodcock season in the spring, the whistling for plover, and what the marshes were like where mills now grow?

Well, while some of us can still carry Ed's old Baker and and George's LeFever we'll have the pleasure of re-membering the day when these old tools were once new, and the joy and anticipation someone felt at the solid thunk of a pair of 6's dropped in these now pitted and hand-worn barrels.

Call the dogs back from behind the doors of time. I hear the wagon coming for us and I look forward to the ride. No need to rush—they'll have a cup of cider and a pipe or chaw, and start this day off by telling stories of the last. Bring an apple for the horses and a little some-thing for the pup!

Trouble

WE LOST a little puppy the other day to a speeding car. And a lot of the magic has disappeared from the kitchen where she ruled the roost. Whoever said "you can't buy happiness" forgot little puppies. "Trouble" was a tiny package crammed to overflowing with mischief, charm, excitement, curiosity and affection. She scattered love around our house the way the wind scatters leaves. The empty voids in space are not one whit more vast than the little corner by the stove where the puppy slept—when the puppy's sleeping somewhere else forever.

Another Daisy

IT WAS CLOSE to Christmas, and that's why I think I had the whole wrong attitude. Bird hunting was far from my mind; our season was over for all practical purposes, and I had a lot of other things I was involved with. So when he drove down my lane in his pickup I was bothered by the intrusion and impatient for him to go.

He was anxious to chat about bird shooting and dogs and settled in oblivious or uncaring about my mood. He talked about his past season and, as usual, bragged heavily about his current crop of bird dogs. He was a Southern itinerant who did some mysterious thing for a living between bird seasons, but whatever it was he did, it seemed profitable enough because he always had a fairly new high-grade Browning 20-bore to show me and he affected exotic leather cowboy boots that were handmade and worth more than I would venture to guess.

I had seen several of his dogs in the field—he'd put them down on my farm before to show me how well they worked—and every one I'd seen was as close to perfection as I could imagine a dog to be. He would virtually never raise his voice above a whisper—just a tiny, almost imperceptible whistle every now and then, and the results were immediate and precise. Once he'd brought a dog he was trying to sell and put it down in an 8- or 10-acre section and the dog pointed and held at least six pheasants in about 15 minutes. If he went an inch out of his way from bird to bird, I surely didn't notice it. So when he talked about Honey, or Belle, or Duke I didn't question their prowess a bit.

As usual, he had a homemade kennel in the back of the truck and I knew by the way the conversation was going that he was again trying to sell me a dog. All the while he was describing how absolutely perfect the dog was, I was making up reasons in my mind to say *no*. He said that the dog with him was as good as he'd ever owned—and better than most he'd seen—but he needed money and since he preferred to hunt on horseback, the dog was a little too slow to suit his taste. He thought she'd be perfect for my walking-around gunning.

By now I'd calmed down, knowing that I was stuck with him for a few hours anyway, and he'd gotten my curiosity up to where I agreed to put the dog down in the section beyond the corn and watch her work. I knew there'd be a pheasant there late in the afternoon and I also knew that she'd never worked a pheasant before, so I was more than anxious to see what would happen.

I have, in more than twenty years of fooling around with all sorts of field dogs, seen it all. There have been the picture book paragons who were worthless and the snipe-nosed, indifferent looking dogs who had performed prodigies. But a given breed does have a few characteristics that we look for: a way of standing, a certain air of competence, an elan, a spark in the eyes. We like a dog that looks as if he can do what he was meant to do; as the architects put it, we expect form to follow function. The door of the wood-and-pig-wire kennel opened and nothing happened. No nose poked out. No eager barking. No sound. Nothing.

The owner acted not at all surprised, and chatted on until he'd finished whatever he was talking about. He turned and looked at the kennel and gave an almost inaudible whistle—a tiny expulsion of air that lay somewhere between a sound and imagining one. Then, slowly and tentatively, blinking her eyes at the light as if she had been in total darkness for months, emerged what you accepted as a pointer only because that's what he said she was. She walked into his arms and he gently set her down on the driveway, where she stood looking drained of any emotion—not a single movement, not a minor clue to her feelings one way or the other.

I said nothing as I turned and led the way to the field. At the edge of the high grass she sat and looked a bit expectantly at her master who waved her on with a slight movement of one finger. She made a half-circle to get a feeling for whatever little breeze there was and began a comfortable trot toward a likely looking patch of heavy briers about 60 yards away. As she worked out in front of us I marveled at the way she eased through the grass. She had to be the smallest pointer I ever saw; almost pure white with a tiny lemon disc around one eye and so tiny that I could have easily imagined a porcelain dog placed here in the field for some bizarre photograph.

She had stopped on a rather classic point, a good 20 yards short of the briers.

"Would you like me to flush the bird or would you like to see her do it?" her handler asked me.

Almost speechless and still not convinced that I was looking at a real animal, I told him to have her flush. I immediately regretted the decision because I didn't think there was really a bird there and I doubted that she was actually hunting after being cooped up for Lord knows how long, and because I suddenly couldn't envision that tiny thing forcing her way into the heavy brambles. But before I could say anything she had been silently waved on and in a few seconds a crackling rooster came soaring out, followed for a few feet by the dog who looked hardly any bigger than the cock bird. She immediately stopped and marked the flight of the bird.

For the next hour I watched as unforgettable an exhibition of dog work as I will ever be privileged to see.

She flushed on command and marked every bird's flight. When one of us chose to do the flushing she stood as still as alabaster and even rolled her eyes rather than turn her head any more than was absolutely necessary. When we had finished working the cover the Southerner patted his hand on his left thigh and she heeled instantly and sat waiting our pleasure—only her eyes were different now and the small veins in her legs were pumping with excitement, the only betrayal of emotion that she had revealed. She had the remoteness of a surgeon who is competent beyond any need for assurance.

"Very nice," I said. "Have you ever worked her on pheasant before?"

"I don't gun pheasant," he said, in a tone of voice that rebuked me for even having asked.

Back at the truck he patted the tailgate once, and she flew up on the deck and vanished into the kennel.

Then he began his sales pitch, every word of which I fully believed.

"That's a little dog, I know, but one of the smartest and best I ever trained. She'll work your woodcock, your grouse, your pheasant. She'll retrieve dove and you'll never lose a one." And, as a clincher, he added, "She don't eat too much, either."

"What's her name?" I asked him.

"She don't have a name," he answered. "I just trained her for the fun of it and because it was so easy I figured that when I sold her, you could name her. I don't talk to dogs anyway ... it puts the birds down if you make too much noise."

"I don't need a dog," I told him, pointing to my kennel where four Labradors were barking their untrained heads off.

"You don't have a bird dog," he said, "and you won't see one like this one for a long time—maybe never."

I told him I couldn't afford to buy or keep another bird dog.

"You didn't ask how much I want for her. Just guess."

I hate this kind of buyer-seller guessing because I'm always wrong and this time would be no exception. I had a damned good idea what this dog was worth—"no papers" included. (He had no use for papers and I knew better than to ask; we'd been through that before.)

"It's the end of the season," I said, "and I don't want to board a dog and fool with one for a year before I can hunt. I travel a lot and won't be able to take her along."

"The people you hunt with ain't ever seen a better dog," he said.

"I couldn't take that dog as a gift," I told him, and then quickly added that wasn't really how I meant it.

"Well, if it was your dog what would you sell it for?" he asked me.

I thought that if that were my dog it wouldn't be for sale at any price...and just told him that if I had it, it wouldn't be for sale. His face softened and he smiled a little and said that he'd sell her for $350 and I could turn around and sell her for twice that—which was true.

"I won't bargain. I need that much and you're the first person I asked. I'll get her sold and you know it . . . I just thought I'd give you the chance to own a really good dog for a change." (This he said with a rolling of the eyes at the Labradors trying to climb the wire.)

As I stood there, the little white pointer stuck her nose out of the kennel as though she was taking part in the conversation. Her head turned from him to me and I had to look away. I really couldn't afford another dog, either in time or money. I was field-trialing two of the Labs and that was stretching me beyond reason as it was. Yet I wanted that little dog at that moment as much as I'd ever wanted almost anything I can remember. And I believe as much as I believe in anything that she wanted to stay there with me, too. I had to walk away from the truck where I wouldn't see her. So I went inside and brought out two beers and motioned for him to come sit with me at the back of the house.

As he went chatting on, suspecting my weakness, I couldn't help but wonder what there was in him that created such absolutely amazing bird dogs. I couldn't imagine him either being kind or violent in his training. I knew he was part Indian, and that part was always up front: unemotional, pragmatic, stolid; the classic hunter, as deadly quiet as a snake or a falcon. His way with any animal—including me, had some undefinable magic, and it made me slightly uneasy thinking about it.

I put my beer down and turned to him and said "I just can't do it now."

He said nothing; just stared at me with empty eyes and flushed me out.

Almost unwillingly I added, "But if you don't sell her in a week or so call me and I'll take her at your price."

He never answered me, just got in his truck and drove off. As the pickup went down the lane, the kennel door flapping open, the little white pointer's head came out and she looked at me in a way that still causes me pain to think about. I know now that if she'd jumped out and come to me I'd have never let her go. In a way I never have. For over a month I alerted the family everyday for his phone call which I never really expected and, of course, he never would have made.

I named her Daisy, in my imagination, after a dog I'd had too briefly some time before. And if I hunted with you tomorrow and saw a little white and lemon pointer I'd have to go over to see her, as I have always done since with every dog that remotely resembled her.

Call me what you will: stubborn, foolish or stupid and I'll agree with you. It's only right that I pay for it every time I see a Carolina pickup, every time I see a distant flash of white in a bird field . . . every time I daydream of what might have been or see a white and yellow flower in a meadow in the spring.

Puppies

PEOPLE ARE ALWAYS asking me how I go about picking out a puppy. So, often having done that, I'll be glad to share my years of experience and knowledge.

First, we ought to look at some methods I've seen and heard suggested by others. These rules were primarily used for choosing Labrador Retrievers, but I see no reason why they can't prevail, breed notwithstanding.

One method, and a most interesting one, was to collect all the pups in a confined space. This, luckily, happened to be in my rather barren cellar. All the puppies were gathered here together and a live mallard with shackled wings was placed in the midst of the puppies. The mallard began chasing the puppies, some pups chased the mallard back, some chased each other. The dog I'd kind of picked out for myself just climbed up on an old wooden soda crate to watch the goings-on. In due time, the hen was extracted from underneath about three dogs and given some cracked corn to soothe her nerves. The gentleman with the duck had satisfied himself that one of the big males had taken charge, and that was the dog he wanted. The little female I liked was now asleep on the crate, obviously bored with all the uncouth carryings-on.

Two years later, the big aggressive male was just that—big and aggressive and as hardheaded as a sledge. My sleepy little pal was one of the top young dogs in our local field trial circuit and went on to become one of the finest gun dogs I'll ever own. She still slept a lot but when you asked her to do something she did it—not on her own—only when you asked her. She was a real pro.

Some people like to sort of roughhouse with the puppies and tend to like those who roughhouse back. Others like to watch the whole pack play and see who's dominant. Both methods have some reflection on the ego of the picker, but as a rule of thumb in selection of a dog, it leaves a little bit to be desired.

The most aggressive dog in the litter, if that's what you want, may be tired, bored or feeling a hair peckish the day you come to see him do his stuff.

Another practice is to pick out a pup and put him alone in a room and see what he does. Does he slink under a chair? Does he jump up and look around to see the lay of the land? Does he cry or whine? Does he bark, demanding attention? Again, this might and might not work depending on so many things we don't understand about a puppy's thinking. I agree, however, if you could use a variety of these tests, over a period of time, you might very well be able to make a very calculated guess of what you want . . . I guess.

There is a semiscientific test now as well. You do certain things with the puppy and grade it on a scale of one through ten. Then you have a little test for yourself—graded from one to ten, and you try to match yourself to the dog or vice versa. It's actually a pretty good idea, but you have to be honest about yourself—if you're aggressive and hardheaded you have to admit it and not end up with a soft dog you have half-scared to death all the time . . . or vice-versa.

A man's personality usually turns out to be the critical factor in his selection of a puppy, anyway. It's just that it's often difficult to see yourself as others, or as a puppy sees you.

I'm not above considering myself capable of making

honest judgments about myself—both pro and con. I know my few faults, my tenuous virtues—and those that I might overlook are frequently enumerated by my closest of kin. But I come up empty when I try to solve what subconscious ebb and flow in me seeks out the puppy that is a shoe chewer, holes-in-the-lawn digger, or good

furniture gnawer, with beautiful soft brown eyes. But I'm sure that's just what I want. It must be.

I won't say I'm a pushover for a pup, but I don't consider a dog spoiled if you find her sleeping on your bed, on your pillow—because when you tell her to get off, she gets off. At least she minds you.

I never objected too strongly to a dog sleeping on the furniture either, even if I was on it first. And feeding a dog at the table saves all the trouble of scraping the supper dishes into the dog pan later, anyway.

I pick a puppy by trying to figure out which one won't mind sleeping on the bed, even though there's a nice big kennel outside in the fresh air.

I like a pup that's economy-minded enough to gum around with a shoe, preferably one I'm not wearing, instead of those expensive store-bought artificial bones. I like a pup that's smart enough to be imitative—one, who when she watches you plant tulips, may amuse you by running off with the trowel, but is attentive enough to dig them all up the first time her busy schedule permits.

And suppose you're practicing your fly casting in the pond, and your baby retriever sits there watching. Her intelligent brown eyes note that part of the problem you're obviously having is in retrieving the fly line—so being an exceptionally bright young dog she pitches right in and helps. A very narrow-minded guy might take exception—but only a pessimist would say "there goes another good fly line." The true dog man smiles and comments on how quickly her retrieving instincts are showing promise.

To all of us, I'm sure a pup is as good a reason as any as to why we do the things we do. An exquisitely glum and somber November morning with its promise of pintails and mallards is just another day unless you have a pup to take along to play with. We've all bought new guns for puppies, gunning rigs for puppies, leased marshes for puppies—and that's as good a reason as I know.

But if you made me sit down and refused to freshen my glass until I told you the real reason I—and you alike— in all honesty feel this way about a little dog, I guess I'd have to say that there's a lot of little kid still somewhere not too deep inside. And I'd go a little further, while you fix my drink, and say I don't see that it's all that bad that we old dogs still have a little puppy blood ourselves.

What do I see when I look at a pup? I remember what it felt like to run barefoot; to have a secret place to sit and think. And I'm still looking for a dog to run with me when I want to run and sit and think with me when I want to sit and think. The right puppy doesn't mind that I'm not barefoot—he understands. When the right pal comes along—a puppy always knows it.

Just my dog

HE'S JUST MY DOG.

He is my other eyes that can see above the clouds; my other ears that hear above the winds. He is the part of me that can reach out into the sea.

He has told me a thousand times over that I am his reason for being: by the way he rests against my leg; by the way he thumps his tail at my smallest smile; by the way he shows his hurt when I leave without taking him. (I think it makes him sick with worry when he is not along to care for me.)

When I am wrong, he is delighted to forgive. When I am angry, he clowns to make me smile. When I am happy, he is joy unbounded.

When I am a fool, he ignores it. When I succeed, he brags.

Without him, I am only another man. With him, I am all-powerful.

He is loyalty itself. He has taught me the meaning of devotion.

With him, I know a secret comfort and a private peace. He has brought me understanding where before I was ignorant.

His head on my knee can heal my human hurts. His presence by my side is protection against my fears of dark and unknown things.

He has promised to wait for me ... whenever ... wherever—in case I need him. And I expect I will—as I always have.

He is just my dog.

Rocky

ROCKY WAS A TEXAN through and through. About half of him was heart and the rest, divided differently on different days, fell between muscle and brains. No doubt you could say that about most pointers, but Rocky had a lot of that "to hell with it all and let's have a good time" attitude that I have come to especially associate with our second largest state.

I know we all have a picture in our mind about what an ideal quail dog ought to look like. I changed mine to come up to what Rocky was. He was a free spirit, as are most geniuses. If you knew all about gunning birds in his country, fine and dandy—if not that was your problem. You went where and when he told you to go. It helped a lot if you could anticipate all this a little and avoid some of the detours he might find interesting along the way. Not being a rib-sprung quail hunter who can go all day at three-quarter throttle, I learned, or tried, to think the way he thought. It's one thing to have a dog that will eagerly cut the brush country into brown and white ribbons all day long; it's another thing to do it with him, step by step.

To be honest, at first Rocky's looks weren't anything all that special. When you've got half a dozen dogs milling around in a truck, you tend to see them all as one, with sizes and shapes and ticking doing little to help you out at first. But after an hour or so it became obvious that Rocky was the one who knew where to go, how to get there and why. He was the ramrod of the outfit, the top sergeant, the range boss. He let the others work the flanks while he headed for the heat of the action.

I wish that Rocky had been mine, as did anyone who knew anything about dogs that hunted over him. But losing out on that, the man that had him was the other half of an ideal combination. Martin knew his dog, his country and his quail right down to the handle. In about the toughest country I know of to stand out as a quail expert, Martin was a commonly acknowledged master. If you didn't get your shooting with him, then simply, there wasn't any shooting to be had. If you didn't have your limit by noon it was a terrible day or else you were out of shells. And I ought to add, so you get the complete picture, that Martin—at least in my book—was about as fine a man with a twenty-bore side-by-side as it's been my pure pleasure to gun with. I never heard him brag about anything, except maybe Rocky every so often when someone was too dense to realize what a paragon he was working with. I never saw him place himself where his shot would be easier than yours, or even close to it, and yet I never saw him fail to grass his birds. I'm sure he didn't think all that much of it since it was just something he did—the way Rocky instinctively went to the right place in the right way at the right time. I don't know of any better way to put it than the way one man did when I told him who I was hunting with: "There ain't enough marble in all of Texas to make them a monument!"

I've hunted in a lot of places with a lot of people and all sorts of dogs. I've come close to seeing about as much variety as a man is privileged to get mixed up with. As you'd expect, I've had good days and bad—emotionally, spiritually and in quality and quantity. We all have; days we wouldn't go through again for love or money and days that are priceless memories; the ten hours afield kind that were too short and the one hour kind that were too long. You run across men that turn into greedy, bragging know-it-alls with a gun in their hand; others that are too timid to take a tenth of their fair share of shots. Cheaters, bullies, gentlemen, polite, rude and just plain thoughtless is what some become in the hunting field and I'm always amazed at how hard it is to guess what's going to happen beforehand. But Martin and Rocky had it where it counted on that score as well. How I enjoyed their company! They made a day outdoors just what it ought to be and so seldom is—carefree, joyous, and sparkling. They simply took so much enjoyment in where they were, what they were doing and in each other's company that it couldn't help but rub off.

It was inconceivable to any of us I know—the thought never crossed our minds that we could not live such days forever. We sealed these times in the amber memory of happiness and our tomorrows were as our yesterdays—to be imagined or recalled with no thought to the immortal clock or circumstance or chance. Foolish? No doubt. But who among you would have been dif-

ferent? Who would have darkened a minute of those days by even a fragment of pessimism or let reality intrude where it was not wanted? Not fools or children—and Martin and I were both by choice when we were together with Rocky.

I heard first through another friend that Rocky had died. He had been struck by a car and was seemingly doing well when he just suddenly passed away. The enormity of his loss, any loss like that, often takes time to strike its heaviest blow. And long before I saw Martin again I had finally come to realize that with the loss of Rocky part of my own life was measured off gone. My cup which had been so running over once would never be filled again.

How can we compensate for such a loss? We tell ourselves that there are other dogs; dogs as charming and willful and as teasing and mischievous; dogs whose distant brown and white will recall the lost one and replace grief with pride in the continuance of things—that there can be an immortality if we will accept such great changes . . . that we can call for Dan or Patch or Lady with all the assurance and joy that we once felt in another name and another face. At least most of us can, or come so close to it, that only that little bit of memory ever betrays us to ourselves. We carry on much the same as we ever did bringing the past to life, now and then, as a mirror or measuring stick to the present. I saw Rocky as a tragic loss, but not an irrevocable one. We, of course, would carry on as before with a new member of the team and time would help us over the hard spots.

I had planned to write Martin a letter expressing my feelings about Rocky, and by helping him air his loss, help to heal it. I had planned to talk about our coming hunting schedule, a new gun I had in mind, the possibility of a duck hunt with some friends in Louisiana—the small but important stuff that gunners thrive on.

But Martin's letter came first. And with it was the last picture ever taken of Rocky. He said that he'd have to skip the coming date we'd had for quail and gave a handful or so of meaningless reasons—the usual facade of being busy, not feeling too well and the like; the things we all say when we mean something else. He never mentioned Rocky once which told me everything he wanted to say but couldn't. I wrote back saying that I understood how busy a man can get and hoped he was feeling better and that I was pretty busy myself and perhaps we could do this or that when we both got caught up.

At first I was amazed to realize how much the loss of a dog could have affected him. Then I began to see some things that I'd been blind to before. Rocky was really the first good thing he'd ever owned—one of the only things that someone else couldn't take away. Rocky was his to a greater degree than anything he had ever conceived of—part of his life in pride, affection, loyalty and even in his fame and reputation as a hunter . . . and part of his youth. The really great loss that lay in Rocky's parting was Martin's belief that now something like this would or could and was likely to happen again. Martin didn't feel that his life could sustain another loss like that—so he refused to make the investment in time and faith and hope and love. But, to be realistic, none of us expects a dog to live forever. We hedge our heartbreak by getting puppies or other dogs, but Martin never really did.

He just plainly and simply quit gunning. I've tried to explain it and I'm sure I'm right to a degree. And I'm just as sure that there is a lot about the closeness that a man, every so often, comes to with a dog, that most of us will never really understand. We say we do. We might even believe that we do, but we don't—not like this specific man and his special dog.

You and I will tend to say that it's all wrong; that a man should know better; that all our human instincts, our philosophy about grief and what is reasonable and what we can and do live with in that way, teaches us to carry on . . . to remember what we should remember and forget what we should forget.

Most of us will talk about a lost friend; some of us will write about them or create a monument of some kind—when it's a very special loss. We have learned that by coming to grip with the mystery of death we can do a little to help live with it. But not everyone is just like us.

There are a few like Martin. I hear that his guns are gone and where the kennel was is a kitchen garden and a woodpile. In his home you'll find no pictures, no collars, no bells. If the talk turns to gunning he sits silently as if he never had the least interest in guns or quail or dogs. They say he never mentioned Rocky after the day he died. They say he never grieved the way they would. But not everyone grieves.

I believe in tears and sorrow. Martin? No. I think he intends to continue to live the way a man does who has lost a leg or an arm—with the certain knowledge that there is no substitute for that precious part of him. He

will never be the same, and only he knows what it really means to live without.

If I ever see Martin again, and I might, I will not talk about the past, the golden days framed with laughter and tinted with soft shadows that fell behind us as we raced the sun and believed we'd won.

I will not try the door that Martin locked. I'm not sure I understand yet, in my own mind, the strength and power of belief that makes a man advance into machine gunfire to certain death, or face imprisonment or torture rather than back down from a given oath of honor.

But history is filled with their names and acts. I'm not sure that I am strong enough to feel that I am nothing . . . which is what sacrifice is, in a way. I do know that I would not die—even a little—for a dog. But I am in a most curious way given strength and an almost mystical insight into something close to being forbidden knowledge when I ponder this whole incident—I'm sure I've made too much of it already to you; the insecure feeling of balance between reality and mystery.

With some men there is only one code and that is total commitment . . . given and taken. I have to think some more about the part of Martin that Rocky owned— bought and paid for. As I said often, I doubt if I'll ever really understand it, but more and more I hope I will. It's not very often we see a man promise something to himself and pay the wager off even though he knows no one else will care—and those few that give it more than passing thought will come to think him strange.

The game of grouse

IT WASN'T THE SHOOTING of grouse, or even the hunting of it, that first created the appeal for the bird that later would grow into a small passion. What attracted me, even as a small boy, was the ethic of grouse hunting. The introduction to this ethic was given to me in the person, and his trappings, of the first real grouse hunter I ever saw.

His name is not important. Nor is the fact (which I know now) that he was known to be a confirmed loafer who lived on his wife's income—and man who on occasion drank a bit more than was socially necessary.

What is important here is the fact that he was elegant; he had style. He even had a "shooting car." I can clearly remember the times I used to see him drive by on the dirt road that led past the farm. The wood body of his Model A Ford station wagon framed the faces of two or three English Setters, in other years an Irish, and I seem to recall one sad-faced Gordon, his chin bouncing uncomfortably on the window frame as the stiff-sprung Ford caromed over the "thank-you-mam's."

Sometimes he would park out back by our old orchard, and I would stand unseen, behind the October copper leaves of a blackberry bramble, and watch. He almost always wore a tie, an old tweed jacket, and breeches with high leather boots. A felt hat framed his lean and handsome face, and he would often make some small ceremony of lighting his pipe before extracting his Parker from its saddle leather case. One dog was then summoned from the wagon, and as they walked out of sight,

I would hear the sweet click of the breech closing and often be able to distinguish the lingering fragrance of tobacco in the apple-scented air.

My Partridge Man passed away before I became of gunning age so I never even got to do more than wave, unseen for all I know, to him from along the road during gunning season, but somehow, even then, bib-overalled and all as I was—I understood him. And back in my mind, the picture of what a Partridge Hunter should look like helped me understand what a Partridge Hunter is . . . and why he is the way he is.

A Partridge Hunter is deeply into the pursuit of something more than a pound of bird. He is involved in the pleasure he gets out of walking around with a graceful 20-gauge or the like. He is much taken with the idea of days afield in the companionship of similar-minded friends. He is much pleasured with clucking to a tricolor setter with a merry gait or a lemon-and-white Brittany with smiling eyes. And last, but not really—he enjoys missing something that seems to be a brown-flecked sound that, more often than not, scares him half to death. And should he, by an action he cannot explain or commonly duplicate, manage to take a grouse in full flight, he is somewhat saddened by the unfairness of the bird he has coveted from this special fox-grape cluster flying heedlessly into an ounce of his randomly thrown 8's.

The Grouse Hunter is not a hunter. The grouse is not a real bird. The man is a pipe-smoking, dog-loving, walnut-stock-coveting mystic. The grouse is a will-o-the-wisp, an ephemeral creature, a laurel-hidden siren. One must hide, and the other must seek. And the game is played according to the rules—according to the *ethic.*

The real Grouse Hunter wants to hunt grouse—not shoot them, at least not shoot any more than the three or six a season that results from playing the game.

The grouse himself exists to be studied by a variety of ornithologists, biologists, and varied cycle-watchers. He exists in order that beautifully illustrated books may be written about him. He is a creation that justifies the supporting of a kennel full of bird dogs for ten months a year so that the grouse hunter can hunt weekends for two months.

The grouse *is* so we can listen to his drumming, count his chicks, and keep a worried eye on the berries that he likes to eat. The grouse looks the way he does so that he will grace the engraving on slim-barreled, straight-hand, Circassian-stocked, improved-cylinder and modified shotguns with two-syllable names and price tags with a lot of zeros on them.

Where the ruffed grouse is hunted with passion, no living thing is really wilder. Unlike almost any other bird or beast, he cannot be tamed, domesticated or catered to. Man has not been able to get his hands on this bird, so to speak; and, as a result, he is one of the few pure things we have left in an environment that is otherwise carrying all sorts of crossbred, artificially-inseminated, transplanted, and laboratory-raised creatures. He has managed to survive fire, plague, do-gooders, land development barons, and, so far, even the Corps of Army Engineers have not been able to drain him dry, flood him out, or turn all of his nooks and crannies into public recreation parking lots.

The Grouse Hunter today seems to have more natural enemies than the grouse, but, bless him, he too is holding on. And, I note happily, he is even allowed to breed, as I see an occasional young Grouse Hunter in the coverts every fall.

The Grouse Hunter spends his time in what behavioral scientists call the Nirvana stage. His wife often calls it something else, but it is essentially the same thing: a great deal of productive time (time spent by others doing useful things like earning a living, taking the children to points of educational interest . . . etc., etc. . . .) is spent around the problems of outwitting a small feathered creature with an IQ of a yellow perch.

The Grouse Hunter's yearly calendar might read more or less like this:

January: Attend local meeting of Venerable Grouse Hunters to discuss the crafty methods used by the members who took a total of nine grouse last season.

February: Start looking at advertisements for a new puppy from "proven grouse blood that does it all" to fool with!

March: Reread Burton Spiller's grouse books for the fortieth time. Ditto, Foster's grouse book, Knight's grouse book, et al.

April: Take grouse gun, very carefully, to skeet club to sharpen eye.

May: Take grouse gun to gunsmith to have the choke in right barrel opened up 2/1000 of inch.

June: Take six-month-old puppy to secret dog trainer that is known only to a thousand other grouse hunters. Trainer reputed (falsely) to work only with grouse dogs.

July: Take family on so-called vacation trip to areas reputed to have superb grouse cover. Area mapped. Chicks counted. Local liquor laws and prices examined.

August: Order new type of vest from Eddie Bauer catalog. New type of upland coat from Orvis. New boots from L.L. Bean. New collars, leashes, whistles, etc., etc.

September: Get puppy back from trainer. Spend enough time in field with him to undo all the training.

October: Hunt grouse. Twenty-two fair shots at game. Two birds. Have first bird mounted because puppy flushed it.

November: Take long, expensive hunting trip to sit in cabin and play gin rummy, discuss choke boring and watch snow or rain.

December: Treat self to another new Remington, Ithaca, Browning, Winchester, Webley, Savage or something similar for Christmas on basis of working so hard. Send grouse Xmas cards. Get grouse Xmas cards. Get grouse print from son. Grouse highball glasses from wife. New grouse book from daughter. A good Christmas. Look forward to coming January meeting with Venerables.

The annual calendar of the grouse would be somewhat different, but the Grouse Hunter has come to believe that except for the brief time spent in the business of drumming, bragging and dancing, and getting the chicks set up on their own wings, the grouse is constantly scheming and plotting.

How else can it happen that time after time a certain patch of sumac and briers will contain a grouse that never does the same thing twice over a period of fifty flushes in two seasons? No matter how the trap is set, it forever comes up empty. The ultimate scorn that I ever received at the hands (wings?) of this puzzling bird was after walking up behind my setter, locked in one of the very few classic points she ever made. I saw the grouse sitting, head upright and alert and staring first at the dog and then at me.

Was I ever ready! I shuffled my feet and braced for the grenade-like flush. The bird cocked her head and continued to stare at us. The dog backed off a step or two and looked at me as if shrugging her shoulders.

The bird, acting as bored and nonchalant as a shoplifter; very simply just walked away and eventually disappeared in the brush, leaving the magazine cover scene of "man and dog doing it all just right in October," with me standing there feeling completely ridiculous.

I assume that there are easy shots at grouse. I *know* there are because several of my hunting companions, with whose skill at shooting I am too familiar, have two or three tail fans displayed in their study. I have witnessed several easy shots taken—and missed for the most part. But I, personally, have only once in my life had a grouse take off leisurely, in open cover, presenting me with the shot of a lifetime. In fact, I remember it very well. It was on a Sunday, and I was working a young setter around the edge of my vegetable garden. In one hand I held a check cord and in the other a bottle of ale. I know the grouse knew this. I am positive.

Ordinarily the Grouse Hunter is presented with a wide variety of shots during the course of a season. The classics include flushes while you're crossing a barbed wire fence that is three inches too high to step over. Another is while attending to a call of nature. More: between the feet, and directly behind you, from a bird you walked past; while you're struggling for your life in Virginia creeper, honeysuckle, greenbriers or wild grapevines; while relighting your pipe or unwrapping a candy bar. The list is endless and varied—the only commonality would be with the positions of the hunter paralleling the sketches in a comic book whose subject was torture.

I'm convinced that grouse like grouse dogs. The presence of a grouse dog further insures against the Grouse Hunter ever getting a fair shot. A good definition of a grouse dog is any kind of a dog that will be seen in the company of a grouse hunter. The only grouse most grouse dogs ever see close-up are in illustrations in expensive books. I know all about the pictures of guys reaching down to take the bird from the mouth of their dog. I've got a couple of those myself, but I don't expect to be admitted to heaven on that basis, nor would I even like to stand up on oath and testify about all the circumstances involved.

Grouse dogs are never where they should be, and rarely where their human companion thinks they are. And they are never near grouse—except by accident. The few times I was really vindictive and for one reason or another really wanted to bag a bird or so, I used my kid brother—who, while not as stylish as a Llewellin Setter or as sleek as a pointer, would at least do as he was

told, and succeeded in flushing quite a few birds in the right direction. After all, the heavily-hunted grouse has come to learn how harmless a creature the average human being is (that's precisely my brother—harmless and average). The hunter who *has* to have tail fans soon learns that grouse can be driven like deer and goes at his hunting with that knowledge. He might take a dog along for local color, but he leaves him in the car or tied to the brass rail at Mario's Tavern for a couple of hours, if he's serious about roast grouse for Sunday dinner.

Of course, I know that some decent grouse dogs must exist somewhere outside the imagination of fiction writers, but I suspect more good bird dogs are whelped in front of log fires from jars of Jack Daniels than anyplace else in the world.

I say that not to discredit the dogs, but to do honor to the grouse. At various times, the bird has to watch out for the evil intent of owls, cats, foxes, hawks, weasels, and skunks, while trying to scratch out a living. He is ready for "come what may"—the average dog, I'm sorry to say, is not.

I'd love to have a box of 16-gauge light 8's for every time I've walked up behind a "grouse dog" on a point that came up empty and listened to the dog's owner point out pridefully that, "A bird's been here, all right. Just look at those scratchings in the leaves!" Well, hell, *I* could have told him that. I could also have told him that you can't serve cranberry sauce with scratchings in the leaves. And while a grouse may now and then let me blunder up on him because I probably sound like nothing else he's ever heard before, he isn't likely to sit there forever waiting for Appalachia's Smoky Josephine, who sounds like a herd of fox huffing and puffing, to do her act.

But grouse, like editors, do make the odd mistake, and every so often, one fleeing the heavy breathing of Smoky Jo will flush like a 747 and do a turn and bank over Smoky Jo's owner, who with a lucky second barrel, will get a bird to substantiate some highly-colored story back in the tavern. Everybody's number has to come up sooner or later—Mr. Grouse is no exception.

No one knows how fearfully I place these words on paper, because somewhere *out there* are a number of dog owners who are, by now, somewhat vexed with me because I ought to know that last year Old Chief played a major role in the bagging of any number of grouse. I grant that this is no doubt as true as "what goes up must come down," and to them I offer my sincere apologies, admit sinful ignorance of Old Chief's uncanny powers, and yet I must, with Mark Twain, say, "I'm from Missouri—show me."

What you really want for grouse, if you're a serious gunner, is something like Old Sam. Seems there was this car full of bird hunters that stopped at an orchard-filled farm in Vermont that looked so good you could almost hear the grouse running around like chickens in the coverts. The sports piled out and gave the farmer a bottle

of Black Label, and then asked if they could hunt. The farmer, friendlier by a couple of sips than he was at first, told them it was fine by him, but asked the gunners if they had a dog. "No," they said. They all had dogs at home, but there wasn't room in the car to bring any along so they'd just walk the birds up and trust to the Red Gods to smile every so often. "That's a pity," the farmer said, wiping a mist of the Black Label from his moustache, "but in that case why don't you take my Old Sam?" The gunners agreed that sounded like a good idea, and the farmer disappeared into the springhouse, carrying the Black Label, and returned a few minutes later with an ancient hired man. "This here's Old Sam," he said. "Sam's never took a drink, or chewed or smoked anything in his whole life. He can scent out them partridges for you boys better'n any dog I ever seen!" Well, the boys were a little skeptical, but rather than lose the chance to gun the orchards, they filed in behind Old Sam and left the farm yard.

All afternoon the umber hills echoed with the sharp spat of 20-gauge bird loads, and along about twilight they came back, giggling like Girl Scouts. Each one had a limit of birds, and this filled them with such enormous goodwill that they pressed another bottle of Jack Daniels on the farmer, tucked a few dollars into Old Sam's bib overalls, and with promises to return soon, they left.

Of course no one at the meeting of the Venerables believed a word of it, so lots were drawn, and a new group of hunters headed back toward the tumbling farm, with the rear bumper of the car perilously low from the weight of shells and the most famous product of Lynchburg, Tennessee.

The farmer was there to meet them, and as soon as good manners permitted, the name of Old Sam was brought up. The farmer took a long pull and, in a voice that echoed the depths of sadness and regret, told them that Old Sam wasn't there. The men clamored to know where he was; how could they find him. "No, you don't understand, Old Sam's up there," he told them, rolling his eyes upward toward the sky. "And, I'm even more sorry to say, 'twas me that done it. Yes, boys, I shot him. Had to. Old Sam got to runnin' deer."

Earlier, I mentioned that one of the best reasons to lark around likely grouse areas is that it supports the constant search for good shotguns. By good, I mean double guns: side-by-side or over-and-under.

I don't fall into the category of being unwilling to pop a burglar with anything less than a Wesley-Richards—but I come very, very near.

In fact, I have been known to take a morning gun and an afternoon gun. The morning gun is often my 12-gauge Webley & Scott, bored improved cylinder and full, and my afternoon gun is a tiny 16-gauge, bored cylinder and modified; I get a little tired and believe that the little gun will postpone my coronary. I do just about as well with it and still have enough strength left at the end of the day to lift two ounces of spirits in a toast to all the birds that we left for another time.

If I were to create the ideal grouse gun, for me, it would be a 28-gauge, 6½-pound side-by-side, with 27-inch barrels, bored cylinder, and modified and choked for No. 8 shot. It would have a straight-hand stock, splinter fore-end, a single non-selective trigger, a non-automatic safety, and 24-line checkering all around the grip. I'd like it to shoot slightly high—centering the patterns about a foot above point of aim at forty yards. And I'd commit two heresies: one would be the addition of a thin recoil pad—not to ease the recoil, but I find that guns with checkered butts tend to slip a little out of the shoulder pocket; and two, I'd have it made slightly butt-heavy, because I think that makes a gun swing faster.

I'd have it engraved with fine scrollwork, a small gold grouse on the bottom of the receiver, and an inlaid plaque in the stock with my initials. I probably wouldn't shoot any better with it, but it would give me a great deal of pleasure to fool with—and pleasure is the wherefore and why I hunt grouse.

On my littered desk is a small bell, the ordinary little tinkler you might find on any bird dog's collar. I ring it now and then, when no one else is listening, and it still sounds the way it used to when my first setter carried it around her swan-white neck. There was a river bottom that we especially liked to hunt. Not because it was birdy—and it wasn't—but because it was beautiful. The way down to the bottom was through a fragrant stand of tall white pines that gave way to wild rhododendron and then some kind of fern. I used to stand there and listen to the little bell solo against the running of the water and try to memorize the sounds and smells so I could summon them up in other places at other times, and they would comfort me. And every so often, right where the rhododendrons started, a grouse would be in flight to give me another sight and sound to store away.

Every Partridge Hunter should have an end-of-the-day covert—a cool place to sit and listen and a spot for a drink and a swim for the dog. It's a nice quiet place to dress a bird, if you have one, and if not—why, no matter at all. You can sit a minute or two and sort things out, watch a worry or so wash away in the stream, and discover that the end of one hunt is the beginning of another.

No one will fault you if you make the harmless wish that you could follow the tinkle of this dog's bell through a lifetime of grouse covers, and when it was all done, you both could rest forever by this riverbank, smelling the pines and the ferns.

Every dog
should have a man

I'VE OWNED a lot of dogs who were strictly JV materi-
al, or who, under more strict coaching, wouldn't even
suit up. I guess that anyone who spends much time messing around with pointers, setters, spaniels, and retrievers
is going to get his share of the dull, the lazy, the ones that
won't and the ones that can't. As we all know, the most
selective of breeding only creates so many good ones—
the rest are scattered around for us optimists who probably believe in the Tooth Fairy and the Easter Bunny.

But suppose it was the other way around: setters
who would only do their best for fine wingshots; retrievers who wouldn't give the time of day to a person who
couldn't fling a training dummy a minimum of 50 yards;
or hounds who demanded a man with superior night vision before they'd run a raccoon.

If the dogs did the choosing, how many of us would
be sitting in front of the kennel TV? I can imagine a quail
dog saying, "Well, Hilly has good form and looks like he
can go all day but he can't hit anything after he's walked
six or seven miles, and you put him into tough cover any-
time and you're just wasting a perfectly good point!" Or
a retriever remarking, "Old Gene always seems to get in
the blind about half an hour too late so we miss the good
early flights and he won't sit out there if it's cold for the
afternoon flights. And I'd like to trade him for one of
those Rudy Etchens or Bubba Woods that can hit something. I'm getting damn tired of him sending me out for
a bird that's healthier than I am!"

If I were working for a dog, there's no doubt he

would cut down on my cocktails, cheese and crackers, the odd morsel of cherry pie, and make me run along at the end of a check cord. I'd be slapped with a newspaper for chewing tobacco and have worse done for missing easy straightaways. I'd be restricted to just one down vest in a duck blind in an effort to improve my ability to swing through a downwind broadbill. Even my little brandy flask would go. I'd be forced to watch Ricky Pope gun woodcock and grouse while I was choke-collared and leashed so I wouldn't spoil his shooting.

No doubt a dog is as entitled to a good owner as the other way around. One friend of mine would be forced to carry about ten pounds of whistles around his neck because he never knows when not to use one. Another ought to have to wear lead boots because he always pushes a dog too fast in heavy cover. And how would you handle the guy who *always* makes all the dogs "hunt dead" when everyone knows that the few quail he takes home are accidents or someone else's birds? Or how would you break the guy who hunts one dog all day in the warm weather and never thinks about bringing him a drink of water, or the one who likes to "sting" a dog with No. 9's when he happens to think he's running just a little wide?

What would you do with the man who likes to show you how tough he is by sending a dog out in a cold and heavy chop for a wing-tipped goose when he ought to use an extra shell or so and his outboard motor instead? Just imagine what an intelligent dog would do if he were allowed to use a shock collar. No doubt he'd teach some of us how to walk in on a point properly instead of hesitantly shuffling around, and it might not be a bad way of curing the dimwits who think nothing of taking every seventy-yard duck shot they can and then not making

any effort to mark the wounded sailers that they scratch down every so often.

It's not too hard to train a human to open a door when you bark to go out, but it's often something else when it comes to using flea powder and clean kennel bedding. And while humans are generally pretty understanding about needing to play once in a while, why can't they get it through their thick heads that a dog, who doesn't wear shoes, finds it hard to tell an old one that ought to be chewed from a new one that shouldn't. It seems that people are basically inconsistent and confusing; they take an old brown chair that you liked to curl up in and cover it all yellow and won't let you come near it. Do they think yellow is bad for a dog, or what? And while most dogs are pretty good about letting humans pet them and scratch their necks, others think it's undignified or demeaning—not the right thing in a decent working relationship.

Then there's that old question about people thinking a dog ought to be "tough." To a lot of them, "tough" means the same thing as cold, uncomfortable, poorly fed and ill-housed. Others think it means a lot of shouting and whipping—as if being relatively small and defenseless isn't enough to show who's who. Dogs want to like the people they're with; it always makes for a better partnership. But it doesn't always work out that way, through gaps in communication and a lack of effort understanding each other's needs and wants.

Naturally a dog wants a good shot, but he can appreciate why a man can't get out everyday and practice and that we all have our ups and downs. There's even a saying amongst dogs that "the sun don't shine on the same man's rear end every day." It's hard for a dog to figure out a man who wants a companion to always be perfect, but does so little to improve himself in the field. If a duck hunter makes such a fuss about a retriever getting caught up in a decoy line every so often, why doesn't he lay them out with a little room between them once in a while? Or if he can see you're working a running bird that only stops for a second or so, why doesn't he move up a little faster instead of blaming you for flushing one out of range? There's no law against a man having some bird sense, too.

And wind! You'd think that only one gunner in a hundred even knew that there was such a thing. It's more often than not a different thing on the ground than it is way up in the air. But when a man gets it into his head to hunt a cover so that he ends up no more than ten feet from the car—no matter what the wind says about how to hunt it—your average dog is in for a bad day. And this is usually the same guy who won't even give you half a sandwich after you've spent the whole morning trying your best to keep him from looking like a fool.

The guy who wants every bird retrieved *just so* ought to mix it up with a big cock pheasant in the briers once a year so he'll remember what can go on, or try to get a handle on a Canada goose that's more mad than hurt. Most dogs don't really mind retrieving if they can get some common sense into an owner's head. *You* spend fifteen minutes or so in ice water, playing hide-and-seek with a diving black duck, and see how fussy you are about where you take a hold!

Well, a dog could go on and on about our faults. Books could be written about what a pointing dog or a retriever expects, but the only ones who'd read them are those who already seem to know. That's the way things are. But good, bad, or indifferent, every dog ought to have a man as a hunting partner. Most of the fun is seeing him all tangled up in honeysuckle on a covey rise or trying to figure out where to set his coffee cup when a bunch of mallards appear out of nowhere. Only a man is so appreciative of a little devotion; he'll put himself through almost anything for a good dog—and even if the dog isn't exactly the talk of the gun club, the right man will brag him up and make him feel like he's a million-dollar, once-in-a-lifetime pal.

There's another old saying that "every dog deserves at least one good man." Well, here's one that knows he's not the kind a dog would brag on too heavy, but I'm loyal, faithful, and loving, and hope it isn't too much to ask that my dog looks the other way every once in a while. I've got an old brown chair that's just right to curl up in and, if my back's not bothering me, I love to get down on the floor and play. All I need is someone to take me out when the woodcock flights are in (or we hope they are), or to sit with me in a duck blind and help scan the skies. I'll always have a sandwich for you in my paper bag, a helping hand, and a kind word. We'll be a team, you and I . . . and no matter what, I'll see you sitting in that old brown chair forever.

Of men and dogs and decency

ONE OF THE greatest tragedies is to see a man who is undeserving of a good dog own a great one. I don't mean the circumstance of an indifferent bird hunter running a superb pointer—that's at worst an injustice or inequity. I mean the situation where a man who really shouldn't own any dog has one that's the quality you or I might see once in a lifetime.

As an example, I once gunned with a fairly well-known waterfowl guide who trained retrievers on the side. We were out on a rocky spit of land in a waterblind rigged for Canada geese. The weather was a bit more than on the rough side; it was bitter cold with a mean chop on an outgoing tide. We took a couple of geese in a routine way—birds about to stool killed rather close to the blind. The dog made two routine retrieves; routine, that is, considering that the guide was a professional trainer and the dog, about two and a half years old, was a big, sturdy and seemingly quite biddable male. I remember thinking to myself that this was a better than average gun dog. His manners in the blind were impeccable; he was steady to shot and from the evidence, was a good marker and showed more than enough heart.

Along about midmorning a single goose started one of the tentative circlings over the blocks. He didn't seem too impressed by our calling and I figured him to be a bit blind shy. The guide seemed over-anxious for us to fill our limits and insisted that I take a shot. I refused, saying I thought the bird was too far, and he said that he'd show us how to do it, and fired. At the shot, the bird turned and flew off, faltering a bit, and then finally sailed down in the water about half a mile from the blind, obviously wing-tipped but otherwise healthy. I remarked that this was about all you could expect from shooting at a bird so far off, and added that he ought to get the boat out and pick it up. He said that there would be other birds flying and that the boat would scare them off, so the dog would pick up the bird. I told him that I'd run a lot of Labradors and that I wouldn't have sent my dog out in that water at that distance under any circumstances, especially when we had a boat that would get the job done in about half the time.

But, having failed to prove his skill at wing shooting, he was determined to show us how tough he was by sending his dog. The dog had, all this time, kept his eyes on the goose and was obviously eager to go. The guide sent him out with a not too gentle assist from his boot. The dog did an amazing job, swimming right to the bird and staying with him through several dives. Finally, he had it in a decent hold—considering that the goose was more mad than hurt. On the way back through the heavy chop, the dog (wisely in my view) stopped and rested two or three times on bits of rock outcroppings in spite of his owner screaming and whistling at him to come straight back. When the dog finally brought us the bird and it was dispatched, the guide took out a leather leash and began to whip the dog, telling us that the damned dog knew better than to stop on a retrieve.

I told him it was a shame that a man was stupid enough to punish a dog for showing common sense in a bad situation, and that anyone who called himself a professional ought to know better and have a lot more control of his temper—especially when he was wrong twice. Here was a brutal man showing off—showing us how tough he was by brutalizing a helpless dog. It's odd how often you'll find a physically or morally small man who takes some quirky pleasure in owning a big, tough dog, and then punishes it for exhibiting characteristics the man obviously envies and covets.

The really good professional trainer force-trains a dog. He first chooses the ones that will be able to take it and benefit from hard, but not abusive, handling procedures. There's a huge difference between this type of discipline and cruelty—one benefits the dog and the other only serves the psyche of the handler.

I've worked with several professional trainers, mainly in the retriever field, and find that they never chastise a dog unless they know that the dog knows why he's being corrected. They know just when and just how much discipline a dog needs and can take. A good trainer doesn't want a subservient machine; he wants a dog full of enthusiasm, fire, and the desire to please. You don't get that with the whip, shock collar or electric prod.

The real secret—to my way of thinking—in training a dog is not to let him make mistakes at all if you can help it. That's what training is all about. Of course, the

dog will do some wrong things, but you have to learn to distinguish between errors in the learning process and times when the animal is being bullheaded or willful.

A really good professional has a sixth sense about his dogs. He knows the peculiarities of wind, temperature, fields of vision and situations that make a dog nervous and unsure. He knows that what a dog will do eagerly today, he may do indifferently tomorrow—and why. He would much rather praise a dog for doing something well than punish him for doing something wrong. He'll start a training session with routines that he knows the dog can handle with ease and confidence. He always builds on a base of success and competence. He knows how each dog thinks and he tries to solve problems before they overwhelm the training schedule.

I once had an English Setter who was a total loss at retrieving. So, as unpleasant as it was for the two of us, I spent a winter force-training her. And once we got that over with, she became not only first-rate but did it with pride and a flourish. But the real lesson is that the dog didn't understand my initial efforts at teaching retrieving. I not only had to teach her what I wanted, but show her how much it would please me. I'm sure she felt at first that picking up a bird would end with her being punished—Lord knows why—but dogs do get funny ideas and sometimes you have to do some funny thinking yourself. And sometimes you get lucky.

Very few professionals are content with the natural instinct of a retriever, whether Lab or Golden or Chessie. No matter how avid a dog is, they are still force-trained in retrieving to some extent. When you're putting that much time and effort and money into a field trial dog, you don't want to risk the day when they "just don't feel like it." And that is surely what will happen.

A good relationship with a dog depends on mutual understanding and intelligence. The times I've lost my temper (and there've been too many) because of a problem in communication have been good lessons—and when a trainer stops learning about dogs he stops being a good trainer. A dog is a mysterious blend of curiosity, instinct, desire, and training. Some are slow learners and some are just not learners at all. They are timid and bold at odd times for odd reasons—like you and me. I've had dogs I didn't especially like and I've got small scars here and there to show that that can work both ways!

The dream time comes when some little belly-dragging pup stops in the middle of worrying a mole run and sits and cocks his ears at the sound of your whistle. You clap your hands and kneel down and he comes, all feet and ears, to lick your face. He's telling you how important you are, that he's your pal and willing to prove it, and once more you get just a little misty-eyed and that lovely vision reappears. You dare the dream again: the long retrieves, the classic working of a running bird; the harmony, the understanding—a life and love put forever in your hands. Long after the guns are laid away, you'll remember a dog or two or three that gave a meaning to your outdoor days that nothing else could.

A friend of mine who has seen more than eight decades come and go just bought a pair of black Lab pups. And, although I knew why, I asked him just the same.

"I can't live alone without a dog," he said. "I've had so many, as you know, and I've always hated so to have to put one down. The way I've got it figured now, we'll all still be together when the last season closes."

The lost dog

EVERY TIME I STOPPED, the moonlight seemed to carry the slight tinkle of the dog bell I was listening for so intently. I stood there, heron-like, one foot in the air, afraid to put it down for fear that the slightest noise might mute the one sound I was waiting for. But the evening was a mocking one—I felt I might well have been searching for a leprechaun or stalking the pot of gold at the end of a rainbow.

I had last seen Pat at about 10 A.M. when she had found and pointed a woodcock. When I shot, she broke, as usual, since I wasn't too meticulous on that nicety, and up in front of us flushed a prime whitetail buck. Before this Pat had been at worst a five-minute deer chaser, just a little run to satisfy her instincts. I hadn't been overly concerned, but this time as they flashed through the woods I had the feeling that five minutes wouldn't get the job done. Twelve hours later, as worried as I was angry, proved my hunch.

As English Setters go, Pat wasn't your "once-in-a-lifetime dog." She was stubborn, willful, and vain. But I had trained her to the point where, when all went well, I could get a decent day's shooting over her. But when all didn't go well it could be a disaster. Many days I simply gave up and led her back to the kennel in the station wagon deciding to do the best I could by myself. I guess I kept her out for a variety of self-indulgent reasons: my refusal to admit I hadn't done as good a job of training as I should have; my tendency to spoil her and overlook the little hardheaded acts that usually led to bigger transgressions; and my plain softheartedness in refusing to come down harder and more often—a practice which might or might not have made a difference.

But by 10 P.M. all I could think of was a hurt dog lying in a roadside ditch waiting for me to find her, or a dog in the bottom of an abandoned well listening to my call and whistle and her answering bark tumbling back down on her in hollow, miserable mockery. I envisioned her collar hung on a wire fence, her foot in a forgotten fox trap. Anger and self-pity slowly gave way to fear and frustration so strong it nearly made me sick to my stomach. It was I who was the guilty one now and she the one needing desperately to have me with her.

I sat there listening to the night sounds . . . jet planes I'd rather have had been north winds. I'd rather the horns and screeching tires to have been the night calling of geese and herons. The sense of loss grew. Nothing comforted me. Everything seemed wrong. I felt like a small and simple man looking and listening for a lost dog while an impersonal, mechanical world went right on by without stopping to help or pausing to care.

The next day I told a friend I was upset about losing my dog, but he paid no attention to my grief; dogs are not worldly goods. That night I returned to where I had left my hunting coat with the slight belief that Pat would be there waiting for me. But the coat was an empty mockery of hope. I whistled and listened through yet another night, not knowing what else to do. Anxiety and fear were shoved aside by a feeling of futility and helplessness. The airplanes and traffic sounds made me feel more alone than ever before. I was on some strange sort of island.

I called the police but they showed little interest in only a lost dog. A check of neighboring houses and farms led to nothing. They promised to call if they saw a white English Setter but somehow I didn't feel encouraged. To them I was just an annoying stranger with a petty problem. I was a suspicious character to several, disbelieved by others, and, in my mind, ignored by all.

By now the night vigil had taken on another emotional aspect for I was searching for an unknown thing. Pat had become a symbol as real as any physical being. I needed to find her not only because I was committed to ending the mystery, but because I wanted to take her to these uncaring people and say, in effect, "Here is the dog I asked you about. See how much we enjoy each other; do you understand now how much it meant for me to have your help and understanding?" I wanted them to learn something about strangers and lost dogs and kindness, and caring enough to listen to the hurt of others with sympathy.

There was little sense in wandering around since Pat, no doubt, was doing the same thing, so I decided instead to find a spot to use as a post. I chose a long, slanting, fallen oak whose branches had caught in another tree. I climbed up, rested my back against a limb, and watched the evening mist beneath me like a silken sea. Here, suspended in space and time, my imagination was free to create a scene of a dog running a deer for a day, then, just as she is about to give up and come home another deer jumps in front of her, and then another. Unable to stop herself, Pat is lead into a land she can never leave. I imagined a dog barking and another answering, then a third calling. My imagination flowed freely once again. One dog started barking and then dogs all across the country answered one another in an endless chain of howls in recognition of all that dogs have suffered at the hands of man in the cold light of the moon. I listened for a dog calling my name.

I placed a small ad in the local paper: LOST DOG, my name and telephone number, a description of Pat and the promise of a reward, but I had no faith in it. Almost a week had passed and I was running out of things to do; yet I felt I had to do something. The fading moon was just a twist of yellow like a discarded rind of lemon, making the night seem ominous. I brought a star book, laid back on my oak bed, and tried to memorize the Pleiades, Orion, and Betelgeuse. I thought of the ancient desert shepherds and their nighttime philosophies on the stars. I thought of their naked minds relating the unrelatable, glibly marrying suspicion, myth, and astrology, and trying to find a meaningful place for themselves while being surrounded by nothing except the incredible extension of their intellect. And I was bewildered when I thought how much of it had really worked out after all. But, in the long run, philosophy is a comfort only to philosophers and I am not really one of those incredible abstract thinkers—just a small, cold man lost in the woods being hunted, I hoped, by a hungry, homesick bird dog.

I tried the old hunters trick of imagining what I would do if I was a lost dog. Where would I go? What would be the limits of my endurance? But this was idle foolishness. Pat could literally be anywhere—around the next turn or in another world. The night vigil had lost its feeling of function and I took to driving around more and sitting less. A pointless use of time perhaps, but maybe, just maybe, I would find Pat.

I gave up when over a week had passed. I took the kennel out of the station wagon and avoided going near the dog run by the barn. My family had long since stopped talking about hunting in an effort to be kind to me, but it didn't matter. My own feelings were mixed: a sense of loss, a deep guilt, and worst of all, a nagging uncertainty. I didn't really believe Pat was gone. I couldn't conceive or cope with the idea of forever. I still drove around the area where she had run away, but more like a person trying to wake up from a bad dream than from any real hope of seeing her sitting by the side of the road listening for the familiar sound of my car. People would recognize my car and wave, and a couple of kids knew me as the "lost dog man."

My mind searched for a simple solution. I imagined Pat had been hit by a passing car, then crawled into the woods and gone to sleep, undetected by the driver. It was neat, logical, likely—and unsatisfactory. Other possibilities came to mind but none were any better.

After two weeks the painful sense of loss faded, leaving a numb feeling of emptiness. I still caught myself listening for her bark when I pulled in the driveway, but the empty spots where she used to lie seemed ordinary again and I didn't think about feeding time anymore. I felt better when I reminded myself that she was just an ordinary working field dog, nothing to brag about, spoiled, mischievous—and yet it hurt to remember that Pat was my dog in every sense of the word. She followed me everywhere, slept by my chair when I let her in the house and loved riding in the front seat of the car. The simple truth was that Pat had gotten to me in her own way, more than I had been readily willing to admit before. I felt almost ashamed to be so sentimental. It was difficult to imagine a man my age crying alone in his car for the sight of a small white dog. But it happened, and happened more than once.

This was all some time ago and I've never seen or heard of Pat again. I'm past grief now. Her image in my memory remains like a poorly focused snapshot of a white dog off in an alder thicket—indistinct and distant like a ghost or a drifting wraith of mist.

They say that time heals all wounds, but that's not wholly true. Sometimes we can work around the reality and believe in a hereafter when we have to—imagining a lost dog living with someone else far away—a kind and gentle master who has discovered that she loves to ride in the front seat of the car with the window open, hates peanut butter sandwiches, and will, for no apparent reason, cock her head and stand stock still for the longest time as if she were listening for a faint whistling carried on the evening wind and the calling of a name she still remembers.

When enough
is not enough

LAST YEAR, while packing up after a rather thin week of bird shooting, I told my guide who was helping me get things together that I didn't need a letter from him telling me that "just after you left, the birds really started to come in . . ." I already had more than my share of those. It always happened anyway, and was not any sort of surprise.

True to form, both the birds and the guide's letter arrived as predicted. But along with the tales of how filled my empty coverts were was one that interested me even more. The evening before the first hunt the men were sitting around getting acquainted with each other and the light chitchat was the typical "who do you know and where have you hunted," before it switched over to favorite guns and memorable dogs. Now, as you know, you rarely hear much horn-blowing in these sessions. Once in a while a very special gun is uncased—a Purdey, a Parker, a fine L.C. or a Holland for the rest of us to admire. And every so often a dog is brought in and paraded around as being "better than fair." Most of us old hands know very well that too much talk about your ability with a shotgun or the precision casts and points that Patches is famous for have a decided way of coming back very quickly to haunt, and haunt heavily.

So it came as a bit of a surprise and a slightly unpleasant one to have one of the gentlemen launch into sumptuous detail about his superb ability to handle his matched pair of 20-bore Woodwards—an ability, he admitted, that might possibly be matched by the work for which his English Setter was more than justly famous. He didn't hint, but he flatly stated that the two of them were virtually bird-taking machines; without fault, peerless and perfect.

The rest of the company was so submerged by this long and rather loud self-accolade that the evening was short by most standards of hunting men and it was obvious that the tone and subject had taken a lot of the edge off the group.

The next morning at breakfast there was more of the same. One of the legendary Woodwards was put together, the dog-of-dogs was unkennelled, and the great shot and his companion rather gingerly climbed into the guides four-wheel-drive pickup. The tailor-made tweed shooting jacket was noted and discussed by the others as they left for their first morning hunt.

Some say it was two hours later, some say it was three, but in any event it was long before lunch when they came back. As the other hunters drifted in hours later they were greeted by a limit of birds hung up outside the cabin—four woodcock, five ruffed grouse. Nine empty 20-gauge shells were placed on the nails, one over each bird's head.

The story as I got it later was that this same scene, with an occasional extra empty (but never more than one) was repeated every day for five days. His dog was as superb as he said it was; he never wasted a footstep, never false pointed, never needed more than a word of caution or directional command. Every bird was faultlessly retrieved to hand. What went on was simplicity itself: the dog would point; the man would walk in and flush the bird and shoot; the bird would fall and would be retrieved; the dog would be lightly praised and the scene would repeat itself. Never did they fail to come back, limited out, at least an hour before noon. Never was a shot refused because of difficulty or heavy cover, which accounts for the occasional second barrel.

The guide told me that he was the most incredible wingshot he ever hoped to see if he hunted for a thousand years and the dog was a perfect match. But the strange thing was the effect on the other hunters in the camp. On one hand it's hard to sit around every night and talk the usual "how did you do, how did it go" routines when one man made it all seem a little unreal, and on the other hand there was little to talk to him about when the evidence was right there stuck in front of your nose and didn't leave much room for storytelling and banter. After all, what do you joke about with a man who fires nine shells and has nine birds in two or three hours of hunting?

A couple of the men hinted rather heavily that they'd be grateful to join him one morning, but he always put that off by saying that he didn't believe in hunting his dog more than half a day and that he felt better in the woods if he didn't have to worry about where anyone else was. His afternoons were spent walking alone, reading, and once, after he'd needed two shots on a left crossing grouse, he had the guide throw clay targets with a hand trap for him for half an hour.

Let's leave this story here and think about it for a minute. It's really not much of a story, but more of it's true than made up. You can find a moral in it—something like perfection is dull, or lonely, but that's not the point of telling it either; you can settle for those if you like, but keep on for just a little bit longer.

What of those mortal creatures, real or fictional or half and half, who if they are shooters virtually always have some mysterious, but right, line drawn to the bird. What of the dogs' stolid workmen too blasé to ever run a curious nose through a rabbit story or roll a questioning eye at white flag and a warm deer bed, or run up the odd bird every so often just for the hell of it?

I believe that there are parameters to our sport that are a little different than the foul lines of a baseball diamond, the out-of-bounds on a golf course, or the height of a tennis net. The rules of bird hunting are many and unwritten; good and safe conduct is unwavering, but there are rules that are as elastic as we are willing to make them in the personal day-to-day idea of having a good and interesting time. Long ago I didn't draw too fine a line between the heaviness of a game bag and the weight of my conscience. But I no longer go afield to feed myself or to prove my ability with a shotgun or my mastery over a dog. I go with an ever increasing curiosity, a wider sense of humor, and in search of a changing sense of fufillment that more levelheaded, rules-minded people would find perhaps foolish, childish, or perverse. I am interested in trifling adventures—not scores, comparisons, numbers in stopwatches, or in tape measures.

The freedom that I look for in the field starts right

there and goes on to offer me what I can make of a day that will leave me with something more than a carcass or the most transient satisfaction of making a chancy shot in some heavy alders.

I know now that I haven't laughed enough—at myself. I haven't climbed enough hills just to see what's on the other side . . . or remembered to make a wish on every evening star. I wish I didn't know how so many stories ended that started out with that magic "Once upon a time . . ."

There was a period when I found the trail that led to home with things like maps and compasses. That is a skill. Now, come evening, I'm beginning to be able to smell the paths I have to take on the darkening wind. I'd like to think that this is the coming of knowledge.

Dog daze

SINCE I'VE OCCASIONALLY written about dogs, the way poker players describe second-best hands, I have had readers write and ask for help with various problems that crop up with one of man's best friends. Rather than answering each one specifically, which takes up a lot of time that I would rather spend bumming salmon flies, I'll attempt to cover them all in a general way.

Q: My retriever is a great dog. He's steady to shot, a good marker and is willing to sleep on the end of my bed. The one fault he has is that when he retrieves he only brings the duck to within eight or ten feet of the blind; then drops it. What should I do?

A: The only sure cures that I know are to buy either waders or hip boots, depending on the depth of the water and go out and pick it up yourself. Or, if you think the distance is critical, move the blind eight or ten feet.

Q: I just can't seem to really housebreak my English Setter. I've tried putting newspapers on the floor but she won't use them. I'm at my wits end!

A: Don't panic. I thought that Zern was at his wits end years ago, but he's still going strong.

Q: Our Brittany is beautifully mannered except for one thing. She chews the upholstery in the front of our station wagon. What can I do?

A: Remove the temptation. The best solution I've found is try to locate some old wooden shell cases or milk carriers. Bolt them to the floor and take the cushions out with you when you leave the dog in the car.

They're better for your back than the upholstered seats anyway.

Q: My Wire-Haired Pointing Griffon is constantly jumping up on me. How can I make him stop?

A: You are obviously a messy eater and he's trying to see what you had for supper. Try wearing an apron at meals.

Q: Our Golden Retriever likes to bark at night and it's ruining my sleep. What would you do?

A: There are several answers to this common problem. 1. Get a night job and sleep during the day. 2. Get up and play until you're both exhausted. 3. Bark at her when she's trying to sleep and see how she likes it!

Q: Duke, our English Pointer refuses to sleep on the floor and has just about ruined our furniture. My wife says it's either her or Duke. I'm desperate.

A: If Duke is as good as you say he is in the rest of your letter, see a lawyer.

Q: My shorthair, Henry J., has chewed through three pairs of good boots—at about eighty dollars a pair. I'm going broke. Help!

A: I wish some of the other problems were as simple as this one. Most shorthairs are a little snobby—try buying cheap boots.

Q: I've read that you can train a dog with a fly rod and wing. Is this true?

A: Absolutely not! Unless you want a dog that points things like Zern.

Q: I've heard lots of stories at hunting camps about great grouse dogs—dogs that never "bumped" a bird, retrieved two at once and things like that. My question is what makes a grouse dog great?

A: At most of the hunting camps it's Jack Daniels or Wild Turkey.

Q: What do you call a dog that constantly flushes birds out of range?

A: You'll have to remember that *Field & Stream* is a family magazine.

Q: I have a lovely little 28 gauge side-by-side, London-made, bored improved cylinder and a light modified, straight hand English-style stock, double trigger and a fitted leather case that I bought because my dog was gun shy at the sound of a 12 gauge. She's still shy and I can't bear to get rid of her. Now what?

A: Send the 28 gauge to me. Collect!

Q: I have a lot of bird dogs, twelve to be exact, and I like them to live in the house because I think that the relationship makes for a better dog. But my wife says that enough is enough and she absolutely refuses to let me get another one; in all other respects she's a lovely, understanding woman. What's the answer?

A: My guess is that she's superstitious. Try getting two more.

Q: Is it true that you had a Labrador Retriever you named Ed Zern?

A: Yes, it's completely true. Zern and I hunt a lot together and I thought that two Ed's would be better than one.

Q: Why does a dog howl at the moon?

A: Don't knock it until you've tried it.

Q: My husband often announces in the morning that he's going to have a little hair of the dog. Since we don't even own a dog, the expression mystifies me. What's he talking about?

A: Same answer as the previous question.

Q: I live in an apartment and have to walk my dog—an Irish Setter. Girls are always stopping to pet him . . . what should I do?

A: Rent him to bachelors.

Q: How do you go about picking out a puppy?

A: Picking a puppy is, of course, a gamble and you treat it as such. In the same way a Las Vegas dice player might let a lady throw for him, I used to let my daughters pick out a puppy from the litters that we bred. Whereas I might be stuffy about the whole thing and fool with confirmation, aggressiveness, and the like, the girls had a much better way of perceiving some aura about the dog that suited them. It was a mysterious rite and I often, but quietly, disagreed with them, however their instincts always proved sounder than my shallow knowledge. Look back on your marriage, if you're married. If you were completely honest you'd admit that the lady picked you—or made it impossible for you not to pick her, which is the same thing. If you don't have a little girl to help you out, don't worry. You'll stand around watching the puppies do what puppies do. You think that they're ignoring you, but they're not. After a while one or two will come over and give you a closer look. Then they'll discuss it amongst themselves. Finally one will start chewing at your cuff or biting your ankle or barking at your shoelace. The selection process is now finished. You pick the pup up in your arms, it licks your

face a time or two and goes to sleep. "For better or for worse, in sickness and in health . . . " never had a more poignant meaning than at this very minute.

Q: I've heard that dogs will point fish. Is this a fact?

A: Yes, even Ed Zern will do this although I've reminded him countless times that it's impolite to point.

Q: If you're so smart, how come Bill Tarrant is *Field and Stream's* Gun Dog editor?

A: Knowledge, talent and the fact that he turns around three times before lying down.

I think that about covers the most frequently asked questions. I checked this list with my old Lab and asked her if she'd like to make any final comments. She put her reading down, settled herself a little more upright on the sofa and thought a minute.

She said, "Can I ask a few questions about people?"

"What kinds of questions," I asked, "technical or philosophical?"

"Well, there are a lot of things I'd like to ask," she went on, "but you probably wouldn't know the answers, anyway."

"Try me," I said. "Ask me one important question." And she did, with that sly and knowing smile.

"If you had one wish what would it be?"

I thought about that for a few minutes while she leafed idly through Brister's book on shotgunning, and then I went to the closet and brought out an old moccasin that she used to chew when she was puppy. I held it up and we sort of smiled at each other.

"And you, too," she said.

Fred

FRED ARRIVED LATE in the spring as if he had had a long standing appointment with us; or like an old and tired fellow looking for a friend to take him in and tide him over for a bit until he was back on his feet again; nothing permanent, you understand, just a little while until the expected letter arrived, or a distant but well-to-do relative came to collect him and return him to the standard of living he was obviously accustomed to.

He was pathetically tired and listless for the first week or so; no doubt the journey had been long and arduous, beset with perils he had somehow, with pluck and wit, survived—no easy task for a rather small Beagle more than a little done in by age and its nuisances.

At first the other dogs more or less ignored him and he seemed to prefer it that way. But as his condition improved and most of the aches and pains went away he would join them in a few minutes of rolling around, then retire to his spot under the front porch and watch them.

Nor did he pay very much attention to me or anyone else in the family. He had the typical Beagle disdain for coming when he was called—or perhaps he just didn't care for our calling him Fred. Now and than he would want to be scratched or petted and would come to me and put his head against my foot and look away into some secret vision of his own for a few minutes. Then having done his duty or satisfied some canine itch, he would wander off and stretch out by himself. I was surrounded by a mixed group of indifferent bird dogs—a couple of setters and a pointer—so in deference to Fred's

age, his refusal to come when called unless it was con-
venient, and my lack of interest in rabbit hunting, I left
him alone to do as he pleased. I had put him in a wire
run to force him to rest, and because of some sentimental reason or other, I had become rather attached to him
and didn't want him taking off to start another journey
of indefinite end and purpose. But after a couple of
weeks I set him free to wander around the house and
yard. He seemed content to do just that; besides, he had
a habit of digging holes in his area that were about ten
inches wide and two feet deep, and I was afraid I'd step
in one in the dark and snap an ankle.

After he'd been with us a couple of months, Fred actually began to act rather spry every so often. He had a
little game he liked to play, and I can see him yet with
his pet toy—an old leather gardening glove of mine—running and barking and throwing the glove up in the air
and catching it, hoping that one of the other dogs would
come and try to play catch with him. Sadly, they never
seemed to express more than the most fleeting interest
in Fred's glove, and after a minute or two of barking and
throwing he would give up and take his glove with him
back under the porch.

Once a week or so Fred would disappear on a personal errand in the morning and be gone until almost
dark; typical Beagle goings-on. But when, on one occasion, he didn't come home for a couple of days, I began
to worry and started asking around the neighborhood for
sightings of the old man. I was very much relieved to
come home from work one night and see his gray muzzle poking out from near the front step. I called him, but
he wouldn't move; he just lay there and banged his tail
against the ground as if he were glad to be home but
needed to compose himself before formal greetings. I

brought him some food and water, and when I got down on my knees to slide it under the porch, I could hear him whimpering. I reached in and pulled him out, and saw instantly that he had been shot in his right rear leg with what looked like a .22. Our vet agreed, but the bullet had passed rather harmlessly through the flesh, and we felt he'd be all right in a couple of days.

Fred seemed more mystified than anything else, and it put him in a rather depressed mood that lasted quite a while after the slight wound had healed. He would sulk around, shaking his head at the unsolvable situation, and he spent more and more time under the porch with his old glove as his only companion. It would be a long time before he would trust anyone again, was his attitude—and I can't say that I blamed him.

Any of us who has owned a dog that has taken a particular hold on our heart has dwelt on the unfairness of allotted time. It seems but an instant—or at best a couple of good gunning seasons—that the puppy we so carefully carried home and placed on the rug by our bed has suddenly become a little dim of eye, a touch slow to get up in the morning, and more and more content to lay in some sunny spot. Somehow, even through the dozen dogs I've owned, I've never ceased to be surprised and a little hurt to discover that today Tippy or Ben or Judy doesn't race me to the door but stands in the warm kitchen and merely follows me with eyes and heart.

You'd think, as I should have, that having Fred move in in his declining years would have made this understanding of the impermanence of things a little easier, but somehow it didn't. I knew Fred was old, but he seemed to be the type that might have been born old and would keep that curious dignity and charming wisdom for quite a time to come. It was the fact that he'd been shot that brought the truth home to me.

When I carried him to the vet, stroking and trying to soothe his hurts—to show him that I cared and was truly sorry this monstrous thing had happened—it was then that I really noticed how gray he was, how brittle his coat, how worn out he seemed, how pathetic, fragile and brave. I felt the thumping of his little heart against my arm; his head, as usual, turned slightly away as if in apology for causing me all this trouble. The tiny hole in his leg encrusted with a dime-sized spot of blood made me think of the calvary, and as much as I tried to think of something else, I could hear whoever it was that held the sights of a rifle on this poor little dog saying over and over "I nailed him . . . I nailed him."

Fred finally formed some sort of obvious attachment to me. Needless to say, I had made every effort to spoil him. The best of the table scraps were delivered to the cavern under the porch, and I found that some of the work I usually did elsewhere could be done as easily on the front step where I could reach down and scratch his head for whatever comfort it was. At least it comforted me, and ever since then I am often consumed with the

belief that one of the selfish reasons we get so attached to our dogs is the fact that they give us something to love and care for which is irreplaceable in our lives—a quiet, understanding, grateful being that is there when we feel the need to hold and love something warm, mute and grateful. I would think of my teasing Patty or Jennifer about a room full of stuffed animals as I rolled on the lawn and played with old Fred and have to laugh at myself.

One of Fred's habits had been to come out from under the porch when I drove up to the house and then bark once or twice—just enough to let me know he cared. He would never bark at anyone else; I was special.

Fred continued to have his restless side. His habit of stopping whatever he was doing and staring beyond whatever my normal eyes could see was always slightly unnerving, as if the dog were seeing ghosts or hearing sounds or musing on thoughts that were beyond sharing with me. He never let me really deep down inside; or believe that our relationship was anything more than a transient one; but that he was in the course of a journey that constantly tempted him to be on with it. Often I watched him pace slowly to the edge of the driveway and stare down the road, consider the alternatives, and slowly shaking his head, turn around and make his way back as if saying, "Not today, but perhaps tomorrow."

And that "tomorrow" finally came. I pulled into the driveway burdened by some large and small worries and needed someone to sit with and sort them out into piles of "not today, but perhaps tomorrow." Fred was always the perfect companion with whom to discuss this sort of thing. He would let me go on and on, knowing that this was the best way—to say nothing and let me work things out for myself. I went into the house, made myself a drink and came out and sat on the front step. The emptiness of the little dusty hole was cavernous; no, it was more than that. By the time I had finished my glass of whiskey I realized that it was final. Even the old glove was gone, and I could easily imagine Fred inching along, carrying his glove both as a reminder of where he'd been and as a symbol of total commitment to going on . . . all of his worldly possessions were with him; there was no need ever to turn back.

After a week of teasing myself, I rummaged around in the barn and found the old lattice that I had taken out from the porch to paint and put it back as if to erase the sight of Fred's room; closing a door to a place I would rather not have anyone else see or use.

That particular hunting season turned out to be an especially good one, and the one bird dog that had begun to show some promise finally came into her own. I spent almost all of my free time on some finishing touches with a check cord and getting her to retrieve. It was pleasant work and rewarding to see it all come together, finally, to where I had what might pass for a "gentleman's" shooting dog.

Fred had almost gone from my mind and I could sit on the porch with an evening glass and think about him more in terms of pleasure than remorse. In the overall, he had left on good terms, and the loss I felt was rather selfish on my part, and I'd come to see it like that. So I was not prepared for Fred's return in spirit or name when a man who worked for the county road crew stopped by one afternoon and asked me if I had a Beagle who had recently disappeared. I said I did—in a way. He asked me if I knew what had become of him, and I said that I didn't. He then told me that he had found him, shot, lying along the edge of the road and had buried him, not knowing at the time that he was my dog.

I couldn't think of anything to say. I never could and still can't. Death has a way of affecting my mind for a while and I seem forever falling short of finding any way to take it all in and make sense of it. But after a minute or so I thanked him for his kindness toward the dog and his courtesy of coming by. He asked me if I wanted to know who did it and I thought about that and remembering a red rage I felt once during a long ago war, I said I'd rather not know. He seemed a little surprised, but I didn't feel I wanted to explain; I didn't feel I could—I didn't understand it myself—it just sort of came out. He said, "Okay," in a way that embarrassed me and got back in his truck. He started the motor, rolled the window down and held out an old leather glove. "This yours?" he asked. I took it, wordlessly, and he drove off.

I went back and sat on the front step, trying not to think and not having much luck. My wife came out and asked who had stopped by in the truck. I couldn't say anything to her but I held up the glove. "I'm glad to have that," she said and took it from me and pushed it under the lattice and went back into the house. She came back in a minute or two and handed me a glass and went away again. I sat there and watched the sun go down, and off in the shallow part of the sky where the weakening yellow was being pushed back by the dark, I saw the evening star and I made a wish. It had been a long time since I had done a thing like that, since I was a kid, I guess, and the difference is that I was wishing, now, for something I really didn't want, since it wasn't really right to wish for things like that, but I did anyway. And I think you know exactly what it was.

A little shaggy

I WAS HAVING a drink the other night with a friend of mine, who happens to be an English Setter. I noticed when he got up to add some ice to my Virginia Gentleman, that he'd been reading Dick Wolters' GUN DOG, a popular how-to training book. I asked him how he liked the book, after he'd returned with the ice and finished touching up my glass. "Oh, it's good all right, actually very good, but . . ."

"But what?" I interrupted. "Every time you read a book on field dogs it seems to sort of upset you."

"I suppose you'll put this down as a simple prejudice," he said, "but I'm sick and tired of always reading what you hunters want in a dog. Hasn't it ever occurred to you that the dog might feel more or less interested in what kind of hunter he's working for?"

I fooled around with lighting my pipe for a minute while I thought of an answer, but there wasn't anything but the truth at hand, an often chancy situation, so I told him, "No, it honestly has never occurred to me."

"I know it never has. And it's about time a few words were heard from the other side."

I agreed by nodding and let him continue.

"It always annoys me that you hunters make such a fuss over what a bird dog should look like." Take Wolters for example. His eyes are too far apart, he's pigeon-breasted, no muscles anywhere that I can see and he's obviously cultivated a second-rate moustache to conceal a trembling upper lip."

I admitted that Wolters was in no danger of ever being mistaken for a light heavyweight champion, but he has a few decent points like character, honesty and the occasional providing of decent whiskey.

"All right, writers aside, take the average gunner. His bird dog has a decent meal for a change, hasn't had to stay up all night barking at the full moon and goes out the next day and points twelve birds. How many fall to the gun?—two or three on the average and maybe four or five at the most. And what does the average gunner do? He makes excuses. My gun was on safe. My foot caught in a brier and I couldn't swing. I had too many sweaters on . . . not enough sweaters on . . . you know what I mean!"

I knew all too well and damned near coughed up a full swallow of bourbon in embarrassment.

"Now, what about the poor dog? Have you ever heard him say the grass was too short and all the birds wanted to do was run? Does he ever complain about it being so hot he can't smell anything or so cold and windy there isn't any scent and he gets hollered at all day for bumping birds? No, you don't. You hunters don't know what it's like down there at ground zero. You complain about too many sweaters on! You ought to work ground in a spring run where the air is different every three feet—damp, hot, dry and what have you. And all the time, His Honor, the sportsman, makes enough noise to drive any sensible grouse into the next township. And most of that noise is directed at some poor dog doing his damnedest for some idiot who just happened to once have the price of a pup and enough left over every month for a bag or two of Purina."

"I think you're just getting hot under the collar over the odd guy you happen to run across," I said, trying to get him calmed down.

"I suppose I am," he said. "I admit I never tried to swing a side-by-side on a bird zipping through birches and cedars."

"You're being kind to me now," I said. "A really first rate shot would have brought him to bag . . . and I admit I was chattering to you trying to get you steadied down."

"Don't worry about *me* being steadied down! *I* didn't miss the bird. Talk to yourself . . . and do it quietly. Most gunners have no idea how much that constant gossiping upsets some game birds. I can think of practically a thousand times when a bird started to run from us just because you thought of something funny to say or tried

to tell me my business. Besides all that, chitchat makes a young dog nervous. In the first place he can't hear half of what you're saying and he can't understand half of what he hears."

"I'm sorry," I said, "but sometimes I get carried away with enthusiasm."

"I can understand that," he said, "but there you were, practically *shouting* for me to be steady the other day, and there I was working like a dog trying to cut that cock pheasant off before he ran into a woodchuck hole. When pheasant turn steady . . . I'll turn steady; whatever 'steady' means since you use it in about 20 different circumstances.

"And another thing," he continued after adjusting the cushion more to his liking, "I wish you'd tell your friends that when a dog goes on point that doesn't mean the bird is sitting in concrete. I wish you'd just walk in fast, preferably from behind me, and do your job before mine gets out of control and I have to start the whole thing over, or the bird flushes wild and you give me that funny look."

I admitted I have a tendency to sort of amble in, because as often as not, I try to see the birds on the ground; a man who is something less than a legend in his own time with a shotgun feels that he needs all the edge he can get.

My friend wagged his tail and gave a small, not overly polite, bark of derision and told me, that a legend in his own time that I happen to hear about from my buddies, is a man who never walks around staring at the ground and never ends up late on every flush. He walks in and looks at the sky where the birds will be. He's ready to do what he came to do, not to make some poor dog worry about being shot in the ear or something.

I knew the man he was referring to and had to agree that not much goes by him and certainly not often. I even went so far as to make a mental note to try to do the same thing myself next time.

"And another thing," my orange and white companion continued, "I wish you'd tell the gunners to be more careful with that young Ben dog. He's going to be first rate, but right now he's got a lot of youthful spirit, and he still breaks and chases a flush. And too many times

they don't wait out the low-flying birds and shoot right over Ben's head. It makes me nervous to think what might happen."

"It makes me nervous, too," I said. "But you know how some young gunners are."

"In the first place they're not that young," he said, sort of curling his lip, "and in the second place why don't you put them on a long check cord and give them a touch on the backside with your leather leash when they act foolish. Isn't that what you do to Ben?"

He'd scored a real point and knew it. He lay there with his head on the arm of the chair looking pretty smug while I just swirled ice around and tried to think of something to say that might change the subject. I was afraid of what he'd say about that quick-shooting act in

relation to what could happen to excited Labs or Spring-
ers—but luckily that didn't cross his mind. You know how
your average setter gets to looking funny when the talk
turns to other breeds. He knew that I gunned and hung
around some other dogs but we had a tacit understanding that I would never bring that sort of thing up in our
conversations; sort of like men never looking too hard at
a pretty girl when they're with their wives.

Instead I started fooling around with one of my
boots, the one he'd chewed up a little when he was just
a pup, and that made him a bit embarrassed. It's a little
trick I don't use too often because I know how it makes
him feel. He just looked away at one of the bird prints
I have up on the wall and pretended to frown at the way
the pointer in the picture was standing to the birds. (He
frequently commented that certain pointers tended to
be a little showy.)

He pulled a small burr out from between his pads
and with a great bit of casualness dropped it on the rug
right by my foot. I picked it up and threw it in the fire-
place and then closed the screens the way I do when I'm
ready to go to bed. He slowly eased himself out of the
chair, stretched deliciously, yawned and walked over to
the door.

As we took our little walk he remarked how much
he liked listening to the night sounds and getting a feel
for what the weather would be tomorrow. I let him
chase one frog into the pond, get a quick drink, and we
went back inside.

"I hope you don't think I was too picky tonight,"
he said while I fixed the small nightcap I always take to
bed, "but there are always two sides to every point."

He waited for me to smile because he knows how
much I like puns and shaggy dog stories.

"Not at all," I told him. "I'm always willing to be taught new tricks by an old dog."

He just growled at that and went on upstairs, but I could see him smiling as he took his place by the bedroom door where he always sleeps to protect me against the things of the night that only special dogs know about.

Woodcock dogs

I'M SORT OF BENT in the direction of being a wood-cock dog man. I have a greater sympathy for them than for dogs that can race the wind and win over a Texas plain or a prairie ocean. I'm probably due to come back as a woodcock dog if there's such a thing as reincarnation (in spite of deserving to come back as a distance fly-casting champion or a frequent high-over-all winner on the high-rolling trap circuit), but I have a feeling that that's not in the cards.

Woodcock dogs and I have a basic and instant understanding. No doubt it started when I was personally, being dogless, a yearling gunner just past being house-broken. If I flushed a bird in those beginning years, I was the one who flushed it—intentionally or not. I spent so much time in the bottom covers and alder thickets that I got relatively good at the whole game. I can't claim a choke-bore nose, but I did have a pretty good feeling for where a bird or so might lie, and I did better, given my overeagerness and inadequate wingshooting technique, than you might suppose.

No one in his right mind would have counted on me to produce a limit; no one would have preferred my company to any but the most ancient or hopeless of bird dogs. But all I had was me, and that had to do. In my favor, if memory isn't being too generous with the facts, was a thickheadedness that no cover could deter. No bramble was too dense, no swamp too wet, no hillside too steep. If it looked or felt or hinted at being birdy, I would plunge right in. I must have flushed unknown, unseen, and unheard by me—hundreds for every one I threw a rather random load of light 8's at, but my options were just two: my way or nothing.

Aside from being a less-than-spectacular wingshot, combined with a certain lack of stealth, I had other shortcomings that even I was aware of; one was the fact that I was slightly hard of hearing—it runs in the family— and another was that I was short. Where a boy of normal size, equipped with better ears than I, would have heard or seen a bird, I was destined to plunge on unrewarded by not even having a glimpse of tawny feathers or the reward of whirring wings and the faint whistle that woodcock so ofter make when flushed.

You don't have to be Nick the Greek or an old hand from Vegas to figure the odds on a short, slightly deaf, noisy boy sneaking up on enough birds to provide much of a family feast. That I did get enough birds every season to keep my interest at a ridiculously high level has to say something about the number of birds in my old covers and my ability to play a little loose with the facts about my hunting skills. You could put me down as some kind of an unreasonable optimist; what would it cost you to be kind?

"Years later," as they used to head chapters in old novels, the boy has grown somewhat taller and a lot more circumspect about ramming headfirst through the greenbriers. Constant pipe smoking has taken the edge off his wind and a little practice has brought him up a shade from the absolute dregs of shotgun pointing. He has, by this time, read a great deal more on the sport, and has had an opportunity or two to gun behind a four-legged bird dog; while not a fountain of lore, he is way past where we last saw him—peering upward through short brush with one hand cupped behind his better ear. While his skills and his eagerness are still incredibly far apart, he shows signs of promise.

In time, as you have no doubt guessed, he acquires a bird dog—a nice dog; a dog who likes him and vows to do her best; a dog who thoroughly enjoys wallowing in the mud of bottom covers, creeping through alders, and jogging in the relative open of birches. A perfect match, this man and dog; for although willing to please, she is somewhat cold-nosed, a touch hard of hearing, and irritatingly stubborn. But they find more birds together than he ever did alone (not all that many by more reasonable standards, but a definite improvement).

Well, more dogs come and go. Shotguns are traded. Skeet and trap guns are acquired. His circle of gunning companions grows. The time actually arrives when he has a biddable, knowing bird dog. His clay target scores are not the lowest in the club every Sunday. He has lost little or none of his fondness for creekside covers, and the pungent odors of the bog country are still as attractive as ever. He has matured, at least as much as a woodcock hunter ever does.

He is at the time of his life where the coming season is anticipated as much for the little picture it will leave him to pleasure over as it is for the actual gunning itself. He remembers what October smells like as early as August. He pleasures himself by imagining the coming opening day to be a bit on the crisp side and it having rained heavily about four or five days before—to clear the air, to damp the bottoms and to thin the leaves.

He remembers an evening bird he saw the last time out in late November past. He remembers swinging through its flight with an empty 20 gauge, a limit of woodcock snugging his shooting vest comfortably across his shoulders. He even imagines hearing its whistle.

He sits and recalls a very special Pennsylvania hillside where he was gunning with an old man and his long-time setter friend—both out against all common sense and at least one of them against his doctor's orders. Standing a bit above the pair, he watched the tottering dog work out the puzzles of a fist-tight bird in a soft and shifting breeze. When she had it absolutely right, the setter stopped, holding her head high, proud, and elegant. The old man walked over, shuffled the leaves with his boot, and watched the woodcock shuttle up through the trees.

"Forget the safety, Carl?" came the watcher's voice from up on the hillside.

"You'd think I'd know better, wouldn't you, after all

these years," answered the man down in the swale.

The man on the hillside, the watcher, didn't say anything more. He knew better, too—after all these years.

He delights in that picture. It's his absolute favorite—so far. He wonders, rather idly, if anything nearly that sweet is likely to occur this coming season. He knows, now, that it doesn't matter at all.

Pepper

NO ONE I ever knew ever admitted, in those late gray hours when the fire wants you to leave it alone so it can go out, to owning the best gun he ever saw, the best dog he ever saw or the prettiest woman he ever saw. At least nobody I've known.

I shot the best gun I ever saw—one time. It was a single-barrel A.H. Fox, from Philadelphia. The man who owned it bought it for one hundred and fifty dollars and added it to his collection of over eighty fine trap guns. As far as I know he only shot it once, the day he let me take it out for fifty targets—each and every one I smoked right in the middle. I saw him a few times after that and offered him what I could, pitiful amounts, really, and all he ever did was smile. I guess I'm just as glad in a way that I never did get my hands on that old Fox for keeps . . . owning something has a way of putting tarnish on the dream. Owning anything does, maybe. I'm not sure, but I think it does.

I know a few men who do very well in the eyes of their accountants. Most of them are the same as us in the long run—with the same little problems that men have because they're men. Nature and time never single out "rich" men. They just deal with men, and we all get the same hand dealt to play—and as the cards are turned over the same things show every time—sooner or later.

You might get dealt "my" old Fox, for example, and have that followed up by a nasty flinch or a failing eye. I hope not, of course; I'm just doing that for example so you know what I mean. No fancy philosophy, just a simple way of looking at fate and what passes for justice as far as I know; the kind of thing we are always reading about in the evening paper, things that happen in South Dakota or Mississippi. Except sometimes it's somebody we know real well. Sometimes it's us.

It always seems to me, the times I get to thinking about such things, that nobody I ever know gets his name in the paper or even passed around town for anything especially good; I mean really good. You know—the sort of thing that'll make a man in his middle years sleep differently than most of us, without that little cloud sitting right there in front of tomorrow or in front of the day or week after.

It's not that I care that much about having the best things of anything. I don't think I'd always know the best if I saw it, but sometimes you figure you'd like to know what it would be like. I admit I'd like to get my hands on a Purdey for a season at quail . . . not to own forever because I'd get to worrying about it, but just a time long enough to know if I'd been really missing something important all my life—not that I could do anything about it, but just to know; the way I'd like to drive a Rolls-Royce with all that smell of wood and leather and elegance floating around me. I don't mean to go putting on airs, but it doesn't do any harm to sort of skylark in your mind about something as long as it doesn't cost anything or do anybody any harm. I never wanted anything that really belonged to anybody else, either. At least not in the sense of taking something away they'd feel badly hurt about. The old A.H. Fox didn't mean much to the man that owned it . . . it just meant a lot to me. I really feel, even now, that somehow that old single-barrel meant more to me than it had to anyone. It's just a feeling; doesn't mean much. But there it is. Because I really liked that gun. I liked it past the point of being able to shoot it real well, if you follow me. Just a funny thing, but here it's stayed with me for so long.

I never really envied anybody very much, and the way I feel about the old gun isn't envy as much as it is something private and selfish. I guess it's a feeling of waste. I never cared much about being the best shot around or gunning the biggest bag either. I manage to take my share in fair sport and I think I enjoy it as much as most and sometimes more. But if I could do it all over and have just one small wish, I'd be tempted to ask whoever it is you ask to give me a dog like Pepper.

Pepper was a small dog compared to your big-going pointers and fair-sized compared to your English Setters. I believe he was about half and half, and if he could have or cared to, Pepper might admit to a touch of the German Shorthair. Yet, somehow, in him, it all came together just right. You might say he was a very light gray dapple. But that suited me, because that's the color Pepper should have been (if you follow me). It was his particular color by nature.

He wasn't either bold or shy. And you weren't ever conscious of him being around the way you are about some dogs. When he was wanted he just materialized out of a corner, or drifted in from the barn or appeared in the back of the pickup truck. And that was the way he hunted for partridge and woodcock. You'd be wondering where he was and wasn't that a likely spot over there by the thorn apples, and sure enough, there'd be old Pepper working the softest wind just right.

Pepper had the kind of walk that always tickled me. I tried a thousand times to describe it, but the only word I know that comes close is "tentative." He walked as if he questioned everything, a little hitching step that had

a purpose but not a total commitment to the direction
he seemed to be going in. He just drifted along; you always felt he knew what he was doing but that he was
prepared to change his mind if a really good reason came
along. He walked like a dog who had more than just a little sense of humor, in a philosophical way.

I always felt I could ask Pepper to do great things,
undog-like things, and he would have if he could have
ever understood me. But for the time being he was content to do our bird work for us, since it pleased us, or at
least me, mightily, and it was so incredibly, so consum-
mately easy for him to be perfect at it.

To my certain knowledge, Pepper never had one
minute of any kind of training, and less than that of kindness or affection from the man that kept him. Yet I never
saw him break at shot; he would often, if you missed a
woodcock or grouse, sort of step to one side so he could
mark the bird down more clearly. If a bird fell in water
or across a brook or pond, Pepper would take to the water gently, like an old man going in inch by inch, but he
never flagged at it, skim ice or none. He often half
climbed a tree to fetch a bird lodged in a branch; he'd
dig a pheasant out of a hole; he'd work as hard as his
strength allowed to get after a bird in a stone wall.

One of the things I enjoyed most about Pepper was
his variety of styles on point. He did everything on a bird
but your traditional stiff-legged, ramrod-tail stand. Often
he'd just be there and nod his head in the direction of
the bird. Sometimes he'd sit if he had to wait any length
of time for you to come up, and several times, especially
in a field with low grass cover, he'd actually lie down,
stretched out straight like a rug. And often the bird
would be as far in front of him as fifty or sixty yards.

He had an incredible desire to conserve his strength,

and Lord knows he should have, the way we worked him, but I never saw him really tired out. One habit that I always took pleasure in was the way he'd lean on things. If you were just standing around talking, Pepper would lean on your leg, or a nearby tree or against the car wheels. He never bounded out until everyone else was completely ready, then he'd rouse himself and go off to work after a small survey of the cover to see which spot made the most sense.

The man who owned Pepper was one of those strange beings who didn't like animals. He didn't like Pepper any more than he liked his tractor. Pepper was a thing he used to hunt birds. No more, no less.

He fed and cared for the dog with the same thoroughness he cared for any machine that needed fuel, oil and water. And that's just the way he used him. When the season closed Pepper was on his own. Where he lived or wandered was no concern to his owner. When the season was open, Pepper stayed around living in the barn when it was cold, and sleeping in the back of the pickup truck on a feed sack when it wasn't.

I believe the man that owned Pepper hunted for only a couple of reasons, none of them having the slightest bearing on what we would call "sporting instincts." One reason was that he was as near a perfect field shot as anyone I have ever seen. To my knowledge he never picked up a shotgun between seasons, never shot a single clay target. As much as I felt a coolness or more between us, I'd have bet my mortgage on him in a live pigeon match against anyone. In fact I'd bet on him against anyone at any game that involved a shotgun, giving him a few minutes to study what the game was. He wasn't an especially fast shot. By that I mean he didn't pull up his gun and fire in a blur of speed. He had his gun up fast enough all right, because he'd never even consider my getting a shot in turn, if and when he knew he could kill a bird he shot—whether it was on your side or not. He expected you to do the same with him, in all fairness. And he never shot at a bird he wasn't very sure of hitting and he took what I considered to be a helluva lot of tough shots—at least tough to me. He had an uncanny sense of distance, unlike most bird hunters who think so many birds are too far and don't shoot.

He knew his gun, a low-grade Parker 16-gauge, would take a fair shot at a grouse at nearly fifty yards. And he killed a good many that I just stood and stared at—and a good many more that I'd shot at and missed.

I'm not sure now that he really did take a great deal of pride, if any, in his ability with a shotgun or really thought much of it. I believe he was one of those rare men who were just born that way and he never knew it could be any other way—or cared. That old VH Parker was just a tool that he knew how to use; like a double-bitted ax is to an expert lumberman.

He hunted to shoot birds to eat—and that was that. I've always thought it was a good thing he was a hardworking farmer instead of a hunting fanatic, because without thinking about it, and he wouldn't have, he could easily have reduced the local bird population to zero.

That's the only reason I got to hunt so much with Pepper—he had to do chores and I'd come by and pick Pepper up. If he wasn't busy, though, he would throw his gun in the car and come along.

We never had much to say to each other. In fact there'd be quite a few times when we literally never spoke beyond some common salutation. I'd soon quit saying "nice shot" or whatever nicety came to mind when he made one of his many spectacular kills since it seemed to bore and even annoy him. In time our mutual silence got to be rather pleasant to me, since I could spend more time observing and chatting to old Pepper—who in all honesty didn't pay much attention to either one of us. He was a free spirit straight down the line.

The three of us hunted—each in a world of his own, and still together. We each had a strange and different motive, yet we were tied together in our rather odd contract. If it hadn't been that I knew most of the decent covers and had once asked him along to hunt on his farm, I wonder if we'd ever have gotten together at all.

The year before last was the final time I ever saw either one of them. We'd hunted the end day of the season and it seemed as if Pepper was putting on a special show for me. As usual he was flawless, something I'd come to expect by now. His points on the three grouse I picked up were typical—one where he sat and nodded toward a patch of scrub oak; another where I found him leaning against a small birch, his head turned around the bole of the tree, like a man scratching his neck; and the third where I saw him just standing there as if he were half asleep.

As usual I was outgunned two to one and as usual no one spoke, except for my ordinary chit-chat with Pepper, who as usual, took no notice of it.

I let them out at the gate to the farm and something made me sit there and wait and watch them walk back toward the barn. My blue-overalled companion never once looked back, nor did my adored Pepper. Side by side they walked until the man turned away from the barn path toward the house. Pepper hesitated a moment, then turned from the path that led to the barn and began again to follow the man. Then the man stopped, and without a single word kicked Pepper in the shoulder hard enough to roll him over. The dog picked himself up, turned around and disappeared into the barn.

I've always regretted to the point of being sick of myself that I didn't follow my instincts and go, right then, and ask if I could have the dog. It was as if I'd suffered some unimaginable cruelty to myself and had been afraid to cry out; found something in me that I didn't really know was there, and I despised that thing in me that I will have to live with forever—that act of cowardice that allowed or forced me to merely drive away.

I drove by the farm often that summer, each time with a recurrence of a feeling of fear and dread. Each time I was firmly resolved to stop and ask for Pepper, offer money for the dog and have an end to my nightmare. But somehow I never did. I like to think it was because I never saw the man up close, only a distant figure on a tractor in a field. But I know that's not the truth.

I know now that the truth lay in my subconscious, the knowledge that some things are never to be. There are things to be admired but never owned; things to be seen but never to be a part of us; shadows that fall across some part of our lives.

I never stopped at the farm that fall, and even went out of my way not to drive by. But even now, as I hunt alone, I often stop and wait and listen knowing that it's only a cruel trick of my imagination that I see a dappled, brown-eyed dog leaning against the far side of a birch tree, staring around it at me with patient expectation, as if he'd been there waiting all along for me, and me alone, to come by.

Test yourself

IF YOU ONLY change your calendar once a year, around October, we know you're a dog man. You have several guns—a couple of light small bores for bird dogs and a couple of magnums to use over your retrievers.

Your furniture is covered with dog hair, and the rungs of the kitchen chairs bear the marks of teething puppies. You have one good blue suit, one pair of black shoes, six hunting coats and three pairs of boots—not counting waders and hippers for duck hunting.

Your car smells like a kennel, and you keep moving the cocktail table around the living room to cover up the stains on the rug.

Your dogs sleep in your bedroom or with the kids, and the kennel is used to store lawn mowers.

The richest people we know are dog poor. Their best investments are in memories—and promises of perfect tomorrows. The pictures in your mind of Tick's first solid point or Tar's first long retrieve are not for sale.

Your dogs take you hunting—not the other way around. Days are remembered for the number of points, not the number of birds in the bag.

You're about as fond of all the silly dogs you've owned as you are of the few that turned out to be superb. You don't for one minute believe that old saying about "a man only has one good dog in a lifetime." If a man can't find something to like about almost any dog—especially his own—there's probably something wrong with the man.

Tippy

SOMEONE SAID that the only place you can bury a dog is in your heart. That way you can call the dog in for a little chat now and then—teasing it about being a clumsy puppy and looking down at your old hunting boots remembering who it was that put the teeth marks in them. You can hunt a day or so again, together, when you need a certain kind of memory—another day you like better than the one you're living in right now.

There's a big hole under the swamp maple in the front yard that Tippy dug, to nap away hot summer afternoons in the coolness of the dirt; and another one under the dogwood that she would fill with leaves that she liked for warmth and when the weather turned around—she'd come into the house smelling like November.

She was always a lady in the old-fashioned sense; quiet, well-mannered and gentle with an overwhelming fondness for little babies. She was always poking her nose into a crib or a playpen or stroller, seemingly immune to being poked in the eye or having her ears tugged—maybe because she slept with my daughter Patty in the days when they were both puppies.

I might be wrong, but I really don't remember losing a bird that I shot over Tip. She was an exciting dog to watch in a field trial or from a duckblind. She was a marvelous marker on a downed game, rock steady to shot, and when she entered the water you knew she was determined to leap as far as she could—she had style and pride and you could feel it. I'm sure she knew it pleased me to show her off a little in hunting camp.

And she was just as fine on upland game. I'd say "Tip, why don't you get in and hunt that thicket for me. I'll bet there's a bird in there." In she'd go and I'd always marvel how she'd mark a pheasant or a woodcock from a spot so dense. You wouldn't think she could see a flying bird, but she'd be right about where it went a lot more than I was.

It's not really important that Tip was a good dog to hunt over, but it is important to me that she was a good dog to be with. She was my pal. We enjoyed being with each other. I don't know that you can ask for much more.

I don't want you to think that I'm bragging her up. I just want to tell you a little bit about her because you weren't ever able to meet her and now the time has passed. Most of us have had one dog or so that we'd have liked friends to enjoy—and Tip was mine.

It always seems wrong to me that a man's life is so out of phase with his dog's. You ought to be able to enjoy your youth together and grow old together. Fourteen years wasn't enough time for me to live with Tip. I wasn't even ready to admit to myself that she was getting on . . . when she was gone.

But somehow you learn to live with these things and discover, happily, that a man's ability to care deeply about dogs is without limit. He has room in his heart for them all. Tippy's daughter and granddaughter sleep by my feet and walk with me and get mad when they can't go out with me—just the way Tippy did. And I strongly suspect that before too long there will be a great granddaughter tumbling around chasing the cat, adding a new set of tooth marks on my hunting boots and getting up on the good furniture—another Tippy, to be sure, knowing that there's always enough love left for one more.

One day soon, on the swamp maple above the dusting hole, I'm going to put a small brass plate with the word TIPPY on it. And there will only be one of those.

Produced under the direction of
William L. Cooksey, Petersen Publishing Company

Book design by Jack E. Stanley

Text composed in Caledonia by Jack Cooke

Printed and bound by Fairfield Graphics, Fairfield, Pennsylvania